Memories of Auroville

Told by early Aurovilians

First Edition 2022
Memories of Auroville - told by early Aurovilians
Janet Fearn

ISBN 978-93-95460-08-8 (print)
ISBN 978-93-95460-09-5 (ebook)

BISAC Code:
HIS062000, HISTORY / Asia / South / India
PHI034000, PHILOSOPHY / Social
BIO026000, BIOGRAPHY & AUTOBIOGRAPHY / Personal Memoirs
BIO023000, BIOGRAPHY & AUTOBIOGRAPHY / Adventurers & Explorers
TRV010000, TRAVEL / Essays & Travelogues

Thema Subject Category:
JBCC9, History of ideas
NH, History
NHF, Asian history

Printed and bound in India by:
PRISMA, Aurelec/ Prayogshala,
Auroville 605101, Tamil Nadu, India

Digital Editions produced by:
DMI Systems Pvt Ltd, Vishnupuri, Aligarh 202001, Uttar Pradesh, India

Published by PRISMA, an imprint of Digital Media Initiatives
www.prisma.haus, www.dmi.systems

Impressum

Acknowledgments: This book is about the very early days of Auroville based on interviews made in 1997 with Aurovilians who lived here between 1968 and 1973, most of them fortunate enough to see the Mother personally. There are obviously far more people who could have been interviewed and were not, so the accounts presented offer only their insight into the full story. Nevertheless, I hope this narrative of the life of a few of Auroville's pioneers will touch and inspire many of the readers.

Contents

Chapter 1, 1968 1

  The Inauguration 3

    Tapas Bhatt... 5

    Prem Malik 5

    Tapas 6

    Ananda Reddy 7

    Ananda.... 8

    Poppo Pingel 8

    G.Thillai.... 10

  Early Arrivals 13

    Gloria Buffi Cicionesi 14

    Piero Cicionesi 14

    Jocelyn Shupack.. 15

    Michael Zelnick 16

    Janet Fearn ... .17

    Francis Neemberry 18

    Verne Henshall ... .18

    Danielle.... 19

  The Villages ... .21

    S. Dhandapani 21

    D. Kanniyappan 22

Chapter 2, 1969 23

  Land and Climate – Challenges.. 25

    Francis 28

  Arrival of the First Caravan and the Beginning of Aspiration 31

    Prem ... .33

Gloria.. 33

François Gautier 34

Jean-Claude Bieri 35

Christophe Pitoeff 37

Dorothee Hach 37

Francois.. 38

Dorothee. 38

Christophe 38

Prem 39

G. Varadharajan 40

Govindaraj from Kuilapalayam. 41

Poonga from Kuilapalayam. 41

Meeting the Mother **43**

Danielle.. 44

Dhandapani.. 44

Francis 44

Jocelyn 44

Michael Z. 45

Gloria.. 45

Prem 45

Ananda... 46

Bhaga Gabriau 46

Charlie Lammert 46

Christophe 47

François... 47

Christophe 47

Dorothee. 47

Joss Brooks 47

Aster Patel 48

Chapter 3, 1970... ....**51**

The Aspiration Talks.. ....**53**

Varadharajan 54

Christophe 54

Dorothee. 55

Jean-Claude 55

Christophe 55

Jean-Claude 56

Christophe 55

The First School **59**

Dhandapani... 61

Poonga 62

Alok Aurovillian... 62

D. Selvaraj 63

R. Ravi 63

Savitra Lithman 63

Ananda.... 64

Shraddhavan Stuttle 65

Savitra 65

Shraddhavan. 66

Savitra 66

Shraddhavan. 67

Savitra 67

Shraddhavan. 67

Ravi.... 68

Shraddhavan. 69

Alok 70

Savitra 71

Lisbeth Nusselein.... 72

Shraddhavan. 73

Savitra 70

Shraddhavan 70

Savitra 72

Chapter 4, 1971 73

Afforestation, Farming, and Community Building. 75

Charlie 75

Jaap den Hollander 75

Francis 76

Joss 76

Jaap 77

Charlie 78

Joss 79

Charlie 80

Francis 80

Charlie 81

Kanniyappan 81

Joss 81

Lisbeth 82

Ramachandaran from Kottakarai...........................82

Lisbeth 82

Varadharajan 83

Lisbeth 83

Jocelyn 86

Lisbeth 86

Ramachandaran..87

Lisbeth 87

Ramachandaran..87

Lisbeth 88

Excavation at Matrimandir, Beginning of Matrimandir Nursery, and Bharat Nivas.. 85

    Michael Tait 91

    Piero 91

    Tapas 92

    Larry Nagel 91

    Piero ... .92

    Gloria.. 94

    Michael T. 94

    Piero 94

    Michael T. 94

    Larry ... .95

    Michael T. 95

    Joss 95

    Kanniyappan 96

Chapter 5, 1972... 97

Work on the four Pillars of Matrimandir..... 99

    Piero 99

    Michael T. .... .100

    Piero 100

    Michael T. 101

    Piero ... .101

    Michael T. 101

    Larry ... .101

    Piero 102

    Michael T. .... .104

    Kalyamurthy from Edayanchavadi 105

    Michael T. 105

    Larry ... .105

Chapter 6, 1973... **107**

   The Mother Leaves Her Body.. **109**

      Aster...110

      Michael Z. 110

      Aster...111

   Completion of the Four Pillars of Matrimandir ....·113

      Piero 114

Author's Note ....·115

About Author ....·119

Appendices ....·121

   The people who were interviewed **123**

   Some words that are commonly used in Auroville **125**

      Tamil...119

      Sanskrit 119

      Other 119

A Dream

There should be somewhere upon earth a place that no nation could claim as its sole property, a place where all human beings of good will, sincere in their aspiration, could live freely as citizens of the world, obeying one single authority, that of the supreme Truth; a place of peace, concord, harmony, where all the fighting instincts of man would be used exclusively to conquer the causes of his suffering and misery, to surmount his weakness and ignorance, to triumph over his limitations and incapacities; a place where the needs of the spirit and the care for progress would get precedence over the satisfaction of desires and passions, the seeking for pleasures and material enjoyments. In this place, children would be able to grow and develop integrally without losing contact with their soul. Education would be given, not with a view to passing examinations and getting certificates and posts, but for enriching the existing faculties and bringing forth new ones. In this place titles and positions would be supplanted by opportunities to serve and organise. The needs of the body will be provided for equally in the case of each and everyone. In the general organisation intellectual, moral and spiritual superiority will find expression not in the enhancement of the pleasures and powers of life but in the increase of duties and responsibilities. Artistic beauty in all forms, painting, sculpture, music, literature, will be available equally to all, the opportunity to share in the joys they bring being limited solely by each one's capacities and not by social or financial position. For in this ideal place money would be no more the sovereign lord. Individual merit will have a greater importance than the value due to material wealth and social position. Work would not be there as the means of gaining one's livelihood, it would be the means whereby to express oneself, develop one's capacities and possibilities, while doing at the same time service to the whole group, which on its side would provide for each one's subsistence and for the field of his work. In brief, it would be a place where the relations among human beings, usually based almost exclusively upon competition and strife, would be replaced by relations of emulation for doing better, for collaboration, relations of real brotherhood.

The earth is certainly not ready to realise such an ideal, for mankind does not yet possess the necessary knowledge to understand and accept it or the indispensable conscious force to execute it. That is why I call it a dream.

Yet, this dream is on the way to becoming a reality. That is exactly what we are seeking to do at the Sri Aurobindo Ashram on a small scale, in proportion to our modest means. The achievement is indeed far from being perfect but it is progressive: little by little we advance towards our goal which, we hope, one day we shall be able to hold up before the world as a practical and effective means of coming out of the present chaos in order to be born into a more true, more harmonious new life.

- The Mother, Aug 1954

You say that Auroville is a dream. Yes, it is a "dream" of the Lord and generally these "dreams" turn out to be true – much more true than the human so-called realities!

- The Mother, May 1966

Preface

The Mother began the serious work of realizing the dream she called Auroville in 1965, when she invited Roger Anger, a French architect, who often visited the Ashram, to come up with a conceptual plan of a city. Eventually a site was chosen on a barren plateau a few kilometers north of Pondicherry. She had never been there, — and would never be — but from a map she chose the centre of the town, where a lone Banyan Tree stood. There was no road to the place and there was very little vegetation around except some palmyra trees and a few mango trees, planted by the local farmers. The surrounding villages were inhabited by subsistence farmers and the land was severely eroded.

In 1966 the UNESCO representative of the Indian Government put the Auroville project before the UNESCO General Assembly as a project of importance to humanity, where it received the first of four unanimous resolutions of support.

This book is about the very early days of Auroville based on interviews made in 1997 with Aurovilians who lived here between 1968 and 1973, most of them fortunate enough to see the Mother personally. There are obviously far more people who could have been interviewed and were not, so the accounts presented offer only their insight into the full story. Nevertheless, I hope this narrative of the life of a few of Auroville's pioneers will touch and inspire many of the readers.

- Janet Fearn, Late 2020

Chapter 1, 1968

The Inauguration

28th February 1968

After the UNESCO's resolution to support Auroville, The Sri Aurobindo Society (SAS) started raising funds and buying the land and the date chosen for the inauguration was 28th February 1968, one week after the Mother's 90th birthday. Securing the land, making a road, and preparing for the event were huge tasks, especially toward the end, when much of the land had still not been purchased.

Auroville's chief architect Roger Anger at the inauguration

Mona (2nd from left) and Gene Maslow (right) preparing for the arrival of the visitors

Delegates from over 120 countries participated in the inauguration

Earthen pot used to carry soil to the urn

Representatives from the former USSR

Tapas Bhatt

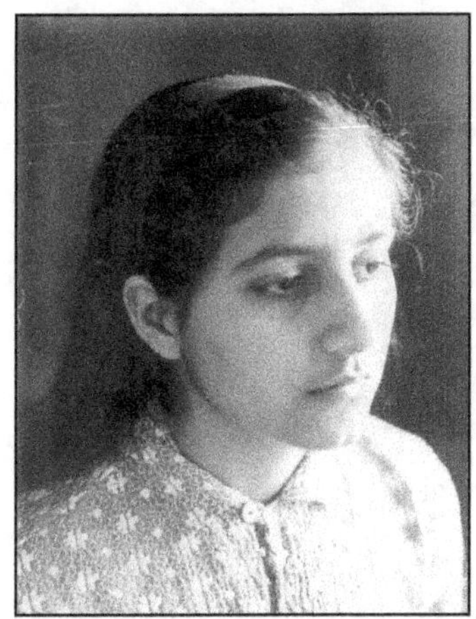

The first time we heard about Auroville was in '65 when the concept of Auroville township was talked about by the Mother and the architects. In our school a professor one day gave us an introduction on Auroville, and how Mother wanted to ask the students to imagine how we would see the inauguration site, and the exact shape of the urn. So we were all given a big sheet of white paper and pencils, and we had to design or dream our own shapes of the urn and the ceremony. That is the first time that I had heard about Auroville in our school.

Finally, in '68 from Mother's birthday date *(21st February)* until the 27th there were preparations going on for the ceremony. I was part of the team, where we were coming up every morning, and coming back home to Pondicherry around 10 at night. So from 21st to 27th February I was busy near the Banyan Tree. We were painting the floral place of the pond near the Banyan Tree, and we were busy with the Tamil village women doing this traditional design with chalks.

On the 27th at night, when I came back home, I had a letter waiting from school saying I had to represent Syria, because the people from Syria didn't turn up.

Prem Malik

On the 27th evening I was in Navajata's (Secretary of The Sri Aurobindo Society) house, where all the activities were centred, and believe me, I felt total bedlam. I was absolutely certain that there can be no foundation ceremony the next morning. I was staying with some relatives here in Pondicherry. So when I went back home, and my relatives asked me, I said that there can be no foundation ceremony. But the first miracle that hit me was that next morning. We were supposed to leave for the site, where the Auroville Amphitheatre is now, and at six o'clock the buses were there to take people. When I left the house and went up towards the Ashram, it was so silent that I said Mother has called off the whole thing. And then, when I went further up, I found there were queues of people, hundreds of them, very quiet and very calm, marching into the buses. I was absolutely amazed. Several thousand people had to be transported to the site of the foundation.

Prem (left) and Navajata

They had come from all over the world to the Ashram. My own experience of the world outside is that, when you have so many people, people are trying to rush into the buses, and there is a lot of noise. And nothing, absolute peace and calm, and all of them were transported to the site without any difficulty. And I was stunned absolutely, because that was my first direct experience of a miracle. I had never seen one in my life. How she managed it is incredible. And then not only were all these people transported there – the seating arrangement there and the food, everything went off so beautifully, as if some power felt in the background was organizing everything.

Tapas

I remember we were all on this bus starting from the Ganesh Temple, and it was a very, very strong feeling of unity, the whole procession of the bus journey from Pondicherry until the urn. For me it was really out of the blue. It was like we were arriving on another planet. There were no trees, it was all barren around, blue sky and a number of buses. Right from the Ganesh Temple, from Pondicherry up Nehru Street past Jipmer Hospital, there were people on both sides of the road, packed for just watching the buses pass by. So that impressed me. I don't know why, but it is still very alive.

Ananda Reddy

On that occasion I was invited almost on the last day because the representatives from Liberia hadn't turned up, so the registrar of our school, Kireet Joshi, called me up and he asked me to represent the country, and another girl from the Ashram was chosen, because there was supposed to be a boy and a girl representing each country for the function. It was way back so I have to recollect my impressions, but still I remember there were thousands of people at that time, but what really dominated the whole thing was an atmosphere of unity and peace. The entire function went off almost in a meditative mood.

Young people from all the member states of UNESCO, more than 120 at the time, were to place soil from their native lands in a lotus shaped urn near the centre of Auroville. Many countries were unable to send their representatives, so students from the Ashram had to replace them at the last moment. Also there were countries that could not send their soil on time. Salt from the sea, which is considered universal, was used in these cases.

The design of the urn was done by Roger, and Mother appointed Vincenzo Maiolini to actually make the urn in the Ashram's Harpagon workshop, although he had never done anything like this before. Vincenzo had to work very long hours in Pondicherry over a period of two weeks to create the urn from reinforced concrete and then cut some two thousand small pieces of marble to size, and fix them to the shell. He was still working on the finishing touches during the night of the 27th. When he finished he was so exhausted that he overslept the next day, and was late for the ceremony.

At ten thirty the Mother's voice was recorded via the telephone line of All India Radio:

> Salut d'Auroville à tous les hommes de bonne volonté. Sont conviés à Auroville tous ceux qui ont soif de progrès et aspirant à une vie plus haute et plus vraie.
>
> Greetings from Auroville to all men of good will. Are invited to Auroville all those who thirst for progress and aspire to a higher and truer life.

This was followed by The Mother reciting the Charter of Auroville in French, which was followed by others repeating the Charter in more than 20 different languages. Finally soil from Sri Aurobindo's Samadhi, each of the represented countries, and each state of India was placed in the urn, with thousands of people watching.

Ananda

Each one of us in alphabetical order came down the slope. There was an amphitheater as a slope and in the middle there was the urn structure. So we came down the slope, and we quietly went up to put the earth, and went back and we put the flag where it was supposed to be in that order. We came out. The procedure was completely in meditation.

Poppo Pingel

I think we arrived two days before the inauguration. We had an appointment one day; we had to get together in front of the school; we had to line up the countries alphabetically A,B,C,D. Sure, it was a funny day and we didn't know where to go. Everything was arranged; many buses to carry us there and you talked to a lot of people, and the people next to us were French people. The French boy was a pilot from the French army stationed in India, and the girl was the daughter of the French ambassador in Delhi. We had a lot of talks. They all spoke fluent English.

We had a lot of time before the buses had finally left. A long procession into the deserts of Auroville; trees were unimaginable. You could see from Auroville to Pondicherry almost, and there was nothing around the middle of Auroville, where the urn is placed. There was no shade except the Banyan. They made an artificial shade out of canvas and concrete pillars, and we had to sit there. The rest were sitting outside in the open sun. It was about ten, eleven, when it was really hot, of course. Having picked up the German soil wrapped in the national colours from the consulate before, we received a small little earthen pot. We had to fill it up, and the girl had to carry the country's name written on a board. Before the arrangements were done we were placed, as I

Curious children from the nearby villages also came, including young Thillai.

said, alphabetically, and it took such a long time as they moved in a really meditative way; I didn't know about meditation in those days.

Roger (Roger Anger was the Chief Architect of Auroville. He passed away in 2008.) was running around nervously so that everything would function. We were thirsty like anything, as we didn't bring bottles with us to drink. They told us there would be drinks available, but we had no access to anything. So we waited, and I remember the Mother speaking, but I didn't understand. It was peaceful. Yes, indeed, everything was quiet, but hot. When our turn came, I served the ceremony with a German nurse stationed in the Nilgiris. She had to take the board, and then we slowly moved into that spiral slope. We moved very carefully, very slowly moved up, and then I had to drop the soil into the urn. Then I was curious enough to look at what was inside, and there was a heap of earth. The others couldn't reach it, but because of my height I was able to look, and the whole audience was a little bit making a haha sound, not quite giggling.

Every delegate got a small little gift from the Mother, a little handkerchief in marble with a hibiscus on it, nicely wrapped, and a small little perfume bottle. And the perfume was called AUROVILLE. Perhaps you can still buy it in Pondicherry.

G.Thillai

Some of my friends told me we should go and see. So I came with my friends here. My village is about 7 kilometres away from the ceremony. We came on foot. At that time, there were no roads. Everywhere there were small bushes, small plants. It was very difficult to walk. I remember the red soil, for as far as possible we could see the red soil for two or three kilometers. And then at that time, everywhere was barren lands and no bunds, nothing. And in some places, some farmers were cultivating crops like millet or groundnut or something. Finally we reached the actual place where the inaugural function was happening. For me it was very exciting. For the first time I was seeing strange people, and I remember there was a huge balloon high up in the air. I didn't know what was written on that, but I still remember a huge balloon. So after that I don't remember the total of what was happening. I was not a participant, but a spectator. I was only 9 years old.

28. 2. 68

Charte d'Auroville

1) Auroville n'appartient à personne en particulier. Auroville appartient à toute l'humanité dans son ensemble.
Mais pour séjourner à Auroville, il faut être le serviteur volontaire de la Conscience Divine

*

2) Auroville sera le lieu de l'éducation perpétuelle, du progrès constant et d'une jeunesse qui ne vieillit point.

*

3) Auroville veut être le pont entre le passé et l'avenir.
Profitant de toutes les découvertes extérieures et intérieures, elle veut hardiment s'élancer vers les réalisations futures.

*

4) Auroville sera le lieu des recherches matérielles et spirituelles pour donner un corps vivant à une unité humaine concrète.

The Charter, in English

1. Auroville belongs to nobody in particular. Auroville belongs to humanity as a whole. But to live in Auroville one must be the willing servitor of the Divine Consciousness.

2. Auroville will be the place of an unending education, of constant progress, and a youth that never ages.

3. Auroville wants to be the bridge between the past and the future. Taking advantage of all discoveries from without and from within, Auroville will boldly spring towards future realisations.

4. Auroville will be a site of material and spiritual researches for a living embodiment of an actual human unity.

Early Arrivals

First settlers Deborah and Bob

At the time of the inauguration ceremony there was almost nobody living in Auroville, except for a few Ashramites who were living in Promesse and Auro Orchard, including Gérard Cruz from Switzerland, who is still here, and a young American couple, Bob Lawlor and Deborah Lee, who had recently moved to Forecomers. Shyama, then Charlotte Neogy and her three children, including Renu, who is still here, and Frederick Schulze-Buxloh from Germany were still living in Pondicherry, but came to Auroville very often. After a few months people slowly started to arrive. They were young people from the West. Some of them had heard of Auroville before they arrived. Many had not. 1968 was a time of great change in the West.

The Beatles had already come to India, young Americans fed up with the senseless war in Vietnam were calling for love not war, and there were student riots in Paris and later in other parts of Europe. Some of these young people came to India to travel and look for answers they could not find in the West. Many of them passed through Auroville to check it out, and some are still here today.

Gloria Buffi Cicionesi

We had just heard from friends about the Sri Aurobindo Ashram, and we started reading books which they had. And we heard that they were planning to build a city, a town. Then we were on the point to leave Italy again. After university, we had been in Finland for two years, because of the high standard of architecture there. And when we returned to Italy, we could not imagine staying there.

The corruption in the field of town-planning and building was such that something within us was refusing to work for that kind of society. So we decided to get rid of our rented flat and go back to Finland. But meanwhile, we heard about Auroville, so we said, "why don't we try for one year?"

Piero Cicionesi

Gloria and I came in the beginning of March 1968, just in time to find the scrap paper, and what was remaining of the ceremony of the inauguration at the centre, and the Banyan tree. There was still the glorious atmosphere of the inauguration ceremony, but practically nobody was in Auroville at the time. The Banyan was standing isolated, surrounded by empty fields. We came from Italy to have a period of trial, you know. We came with curiosity to experience a whole town built on the grounds of spirituality. That was quite a striking

intention, I would say, in coming from Italy and from Europe. We started to be busy soon after we arrived, because the amphitheatre that had been used for the ceremony was actually already becoming dilapidated, because it was only made by piling up earth. It was not concrete at all or covered with stone like now. And that was one of the first things we started to consolidate.

Jocelyn Shupack

Jocelyn (third from left)

I didn't know where I was going when I started. I was sitting in a house in California with my legs crossed under me kind of meditating on a painting on a wall. The painting disappeared, the wall disappeared, the house disappeared. There was a face that emerged from there, and it said, "come to India now." More than a year later I was in Kathmandu. Then as I was leaving Kathmandu, someone, it happened to be Francis Neemberry, was sitting downstairs in the lobby. I was on my way to go on a plane back to India. Francis said, "where are you going?" I said, "Ceylon" (now Sri Lanka). He said, "why don't you stop in Pondicherry? It is an ashram that is like a country club." I said, "is it on the beach?" He said, "yes." I had lived on the beach in Mexico and Spain. I like beaches. So I thought okay, I'll break my trip for three days in Pondicherry and then go to Ceylon.

Michael Zelnick

Michael with Ishita, who still lives in Auroville

I was in the US, and I hit the '60's head on. I had the full '60's experience in the US. Having said that, you have probably correctly assumed that some place along the line, I had experimented with psychedelics, and as a matter of fact, the second time I tried psychedelics, I had a very profound experience, which I can only describe as saying that I woke up, and knew what my life was about, and knew that in due course I would go off and try to find a teacher. I would devote my life to a spiritual pursuit. It took me a couple of years to actually get to the point of doing it. Meanwhile, I had decided that when I finished school, I was going to go to Japan and see if I could enter a Zen monastery. About two weeks before I was scheduled to leave, these guys came back to the US, and they came to the west coast, and they returned to their home, which was not far from Portland, where I was in school at the time. I went to visit them. And what happened is a little difficult to describe, but we spent an evening together chatting pretty casually. They had liked the Ashram, and had found it interesting, but in fact they had never been moved to think about staying there.

They have never been back. They didn't talk at great length about the Ashram or the Mother, but in the course of the time that I spent with them, I experienced something that I can only describe as something coming through them and totally zapping. I mean, I got totally turned upside down. I don't know how to describe it, except I was very aware that something came through these people, and that it was somehow related to where they had been in Pondicherry, and that is where I had to go.

So without further ado, I changed my plans. I had been on the west coast and had been planning to get a boat to Japan, and instead I went back to the east coast, and flew from New York to Rome, and hitch-hiked from there to India. It was 1968, and one could travel pretty casually. One could still pass through places like Iran and Afghanistan without any problem. But I never got any further than Pondicherry, and decided that I would plunk myself down at the Samadhi, and basically sit there until something happened, and something happened rather promptly. I was sitting in the Ashram one day with eyes closed, and I had this inner experience of the Mother passing by. She was wearing this dress with a long train, and as she passed by me the train sort of just touched me, and it was another one of the mind-boggling experiences. That's what it is about, and so

I am going to stay here. A couple of days later a friend took me for a bicycle ride out to Auroville. This was September 1968, and there was not much of Auroville at the time, but we cycled around in Auroville, and came back to Pondicherry. (Michael remained in the Ashram for the next 10 years before finally moving to Auroville).

Janet Fearn

I came in June of 1968. I was traveling around India, and I heard about the Mother in Pondicherry, so I decided to stop for a couple of days. And then I spent one night in Pondicherry, and the next day I walked to the Auroville office, which was across the street from the Ashram at that time. As I went inside the first person I met was Alice (passed away many years ago), whom I had met one year before in Japan quite by chance with her husband Norman Thomas, now Navoditte (passed away in 2020 at the age of 93). So Alice said to me, "you have to meet the Mother and I can arrange it." And I said, "alright." I didn't know who the Mother was, and I didn't know what it was all about, but I didn't see why not. So within a few days I had actually met the Mother.

A few months later there was an American, Gene Maslow, living in the Ashram who said, "do you want to come to Auroville tomorrow and help me build my house?" I said, "alright, why not?" The land-rover that was supposed to take us back to Pondicherry at six o'clock didn't show up. So there I was, and I spent my first night in Auroville, and after that I stayed.

Gene was one of the first settlers in the Centre area, where he built a movable house which Mother called Sincerity, later becoming the name of the community near Matrimandir where Gene's house was located.

In 1972 he went back to the US and only returned in 1996, when he was very sick with cancer. He passed away in the Ashram on 28th February 1996, Auroville's 28th birthday.

At that time Auroville was a blank slate and so full of promise. We had such an opportunity that we felt we couldn't go anywhere but forward. My relationships at that time were with the villagers from Kottakarai. The relationship with the villagers was very friendly. They invited us to their weddings and their ceremonies, and they were very curious about us. It's quite different from today, where we have so much history. Later when I built my house in what is now the Matrimandir Nursery, I asked the Mother for a name for the house, and she called it Joy.

Francis Neemberry

I came to Pondicherry in September '68, looking for a good French meal. I found the Sri Aurobindo Ashram very comfortable and clean, and a good place to rest. Someone asked me to come to Auroville and help them build their house, a gentleman by the name of Gene Maslow. He asked me to come to the city of the future, the city of human unity. I got on a land-rover and travelled over very uncomfortable roads for 15 or 20 minutes, and then it stopped, and the driver said, "we're here." And I said, "where?", because there was nothing. It was all red, and nothing was growing. One thing led to another. I missed my bus back to town and had to spend a night. Anyway I spent my first couple of months near where Bharat Nivas is today in a place called the Pump House.

Verne Henshall

When I reached Pondicherry and spent my first evenings in town, I was welcomed by Mother's all-pervading consciousness. In a very sweet and loving way she welcomed me to Pondicherry and to Auroville. I kind of recognised this person as the one who had appeared to me in a very strong vision or dream when I was in England. Some of the very first new settlers had already started a community at Forecomers. Others built their huts near the centre area, which Mother called Peace. There was also a new community near AuroOrchard called Hope.

Danielle

I was living at the beginning in Pondicherry, and I was told after some time to go to Hope, which is in the Orchard, and which was built by Gloria and Piero. So in Hope there were a few huts in the Orchard. The Orchard was barren land, which struck me also. There was a little temple on one side, which was surrounded by nothing. There were about 4 huts in the Orchard, which were similar to those in Aspiration. In a small hut, one could live one or two, but I was lucky enough to be one. And between two huts, there was a very simple sanitary with water actually. We were lucky enough to have water. And in those huts, of course, there was no AC or fan or anything, but it was cool. We were not too hot. It was quite nice. It was a keeth roof with open windows. People could live there quite well.

The Villages

At this time many of the people in the surrounding villages were surviving on a subsistence standard of living. They were lucky if they ate two meals a day. They had never seen electric lights, telephones, or running water. Most had never been as far as Pondicherry, as there was no bus service and only the well-to-do could afford a bicycle. Very few had ever seen a white person. Dhandapani and Kanniyappan were then about eight years old.

Deborah with Selakannan (father of Dhandapani)

S. Dhandapani

Well, firstly I was scared about seeing these white people, feeling very shy, and I didn't know the language they were speaking and what they were saying. But a lot of beautiful smiles were coming from these people.

Because I was very shy, I would always look down. I wouldn't look at their faces. When I went back to the village, I told them where I saw these white people and all that. Some of the children and some of the older people also scared me, saying that these people might take you away from the village. This was one fear which I had, because it was all so new. These white people were seen for the first time by me, and I didn't have that much confidence.

What were they going to do here? Because they just landed in this desert area with no water, and to go to Pondicherry for shopping you had to walk. There were no motorcycles, no cars, no lorries, nothing. We had mostly bullock carts, so we used to ride on the bullock carts. Yes, the fear that was originally in the village changed very slowly. How it changed was, after staying with these people here, I moved closely with them. It was difficult to understand English, although a lot of words I could understand. And Bob and Deborah would speak a little bit of Tamil, very, very strange Tamil with an American accent and say all the things differently. And I would share my experience in the village with the children. When I played, I would tell them about it. So that's how my fear which was there slowly went away. That was mainly because of just being with them for some time.

D. Kanniyappan

It was really new seeing white people. We used to run away when we saw a Westerner, because we had never seen them before. We were small, so they seemed frightening. They were not dangerous-looking or being dangerous to us, but we were just scared. I don't know

why. Now we are very friendly. I was around 8 or 9, I don't know exactly. I was a kid, I was going to school first, and then I was not interested anymore, so I didn't go very regularly. I came to the Auroville area with the other children, bringing goats and looking around.

Chapter 2, 1969

Erosion and canyons

Variable overset

Verging on a desert

Variable overset

Francis

The first summer, when the temperature rose to an unbelievable degree and the humidity was right behind it, I was lying on the floor of this hut, having difficulty breathing because it was so hot. We had to create shade somewhere. After the first rain when the amount of water that went through and washed away the topsoil that was left, it was obvious that something had to be done. So I just went out and started putting a tree here and doing a bund there. In the beginning, we must have lost at least 60% of our trees. If it wasn't due to lack of water, it was due to the *ammas* out there looking for firewood, or a cow or a goat which saw a little piece of

green out there in the summertime. It was devastating. Sometimes our pits were planted three or four times before something actually took.

Somewhere in 1969 Bob came over and was talking about building a dam in Forecomers canyon and was looking for assistance, both physically and financially. I thought it was interesting and went to assist him. Building a dam is something I never did before. The place was barren, there was no shade. When it rained, we were flooded. Everything went into the canyon and washed into the sea.

You could go to the beach and just look out for half a kilometer and see that everything was bright red, and all the earth was pouring into the ocean. After the dam was built, Bob and Deborah went to America and I stayed in Forecomers. A fellow called Tim Reese came out from Pondicherry. Tim organized with the Ashram school children to go to Marakanam to harvest seeds, and we set up a whole procedure with plastic bags and sand. The boys would do the sand bags and girls would chip the seeds with nail clippers, which came from America because at the time you couldn't get them here. I wrote to my mother and asked her to please send two hundred pairs of nail clippers, which confirmed her true belief that I had lost my mind. We set up a whole nursery and Tim went to the Mother and asked for a name. The Mother gave him the name Success. Success is still an area in Auroville, but it is no longer a tree nursery. We used to hire whole villages to go out and dig tree holes. At the time we were doing one cubic meter. It was excessive, and we would pay them according to whether it was soft earth, or if there was too much stone, etc, etc. We got into tremendous competition among ourselves about buying compost from the villages. The villagers enjoyed it. We would bid against each other, and one day it dawned on us that we should unite in our compost buying. It was an interesting time.

Arrival in Promesse

Arrival of the First Caravan and the Beginning of Aspiration

In the summer of 1969, it was learned that a caravan of young people was leaving France for Auroville on 15th August. It suddenly became necessary to build many houses and a community kitchen.

Departure of the first caravan from Paris to Auroville

Goatherds

Typical village house made with mud and thatched roof

Goats

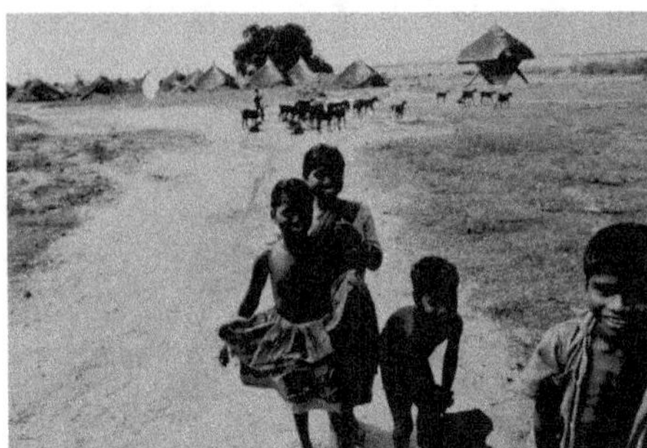

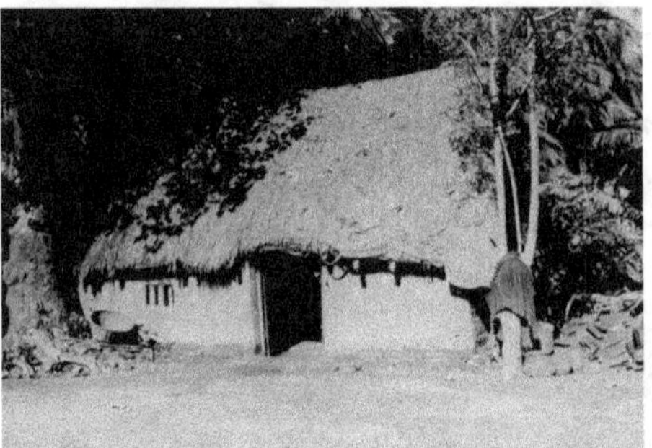

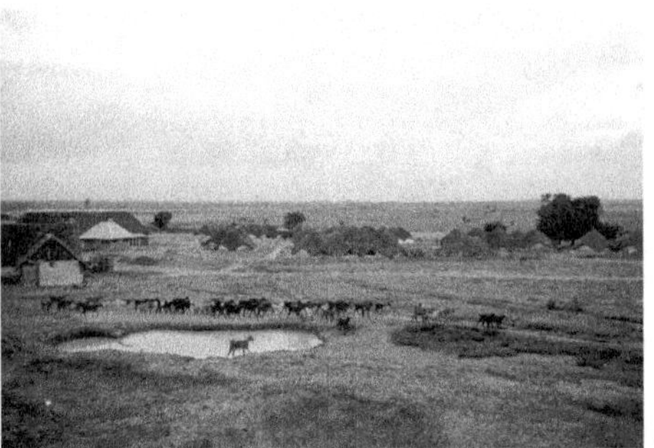

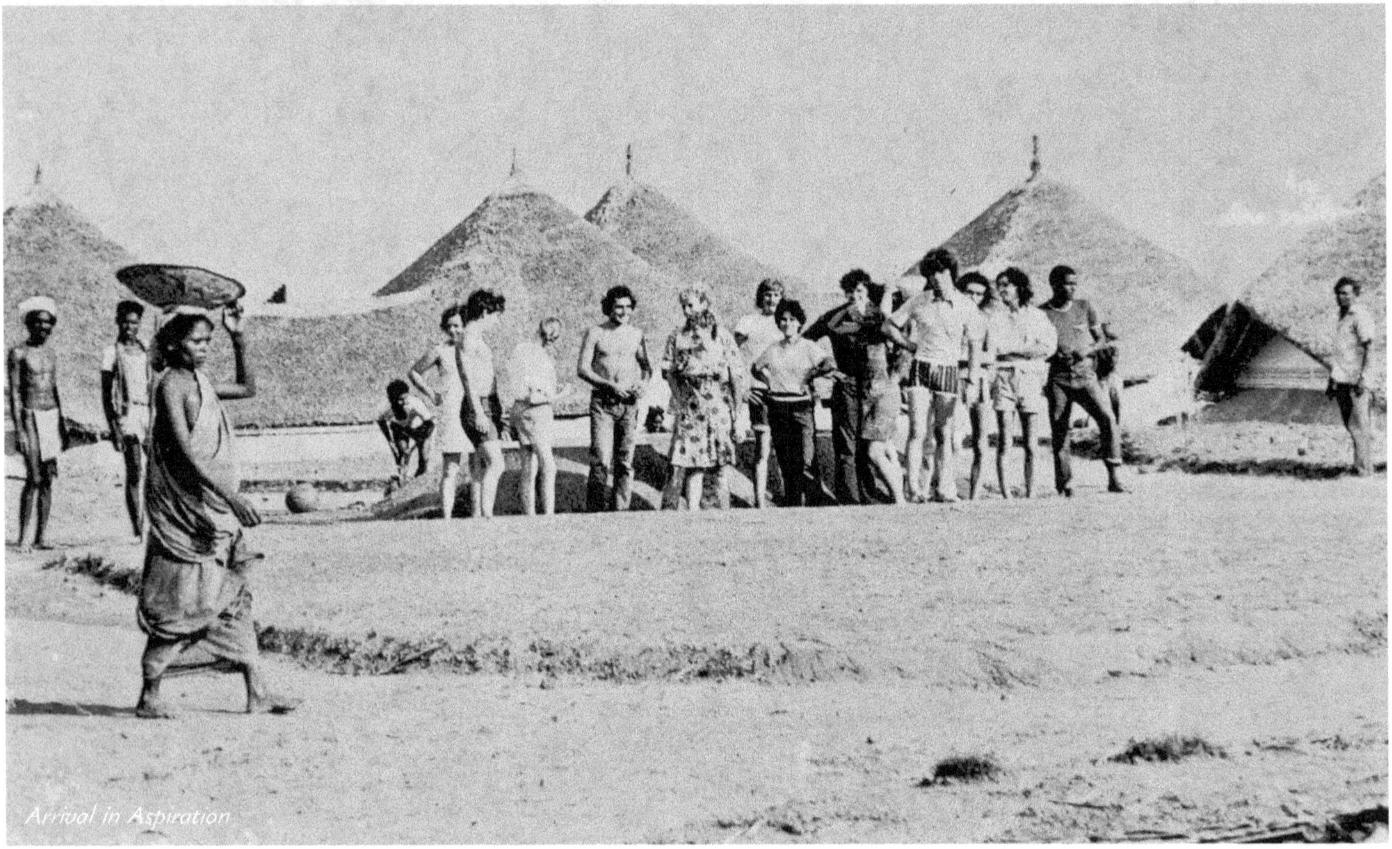

Arrival in Aspiration

Prem

One of the biggest difficulties was there was no place to live in Auroville. And just at that time we got news from France that a group of thirty odd people were coming to Auroville. And the Mother said, "they are not going to live in Pondicherry. They must live in Auroville." We said, "Mother, where are they going to live in Auroville? There is no place." She said, "build it." And then the idea of Aspiration came, only it was not called Aspiration. It was called the Advance Colony. So we started building these huts. And the experiences we went through were absolutely amazing because at the first meeting of the committee *(Comité Administratif d'Auroville known as CAA)*, Navajata, who was the Secretary, announced that we had only Rs. 40,000 in the bank, and the Mother wanted us to construct this colony to accommodate 30 people. How could we do it with Rs. 40,000?

So we went back to the Mother, and it was one of my first experiences of a miracle, because for me Auroville is a series of miracles. It is no planning, nothing of the sort. We cannot take credit for various things that happened, because in fact we did very little. She said you do your work, by which she meant we would build the community, and I'll do mine, which meant that she would bring in the money. And we found that the money started arriving faster than we could use it. It was amazing, absolutely.

Gloria

It was necessary first to build very quickly some huts for newcomers near Promesse, in a place called 'Hope'. We had done a prototype, because in the meanwhile we were requested to build a community in Aspiration for about 80 people, temporary, with thatched roofs. This is not really on the periphery of the township, but closer to the sea, where Roger Anger, the chief architect, had foreseen the first nucleus as an experiment.

Roof module

It was called Auromodèle, like a model for what Auroville had to be. Before that, it was necessary to provide

Inside a hut in Aspiration

accommodation for the people, who would build Auromodèle. So we have done a kind of semi precast hut all with module roofs.

We had a team of carpenters, very nice, very good from the village, and with them, and a team of masons, they started to build very quickly, because in '69 a caravan of French people was expected to be coming with several vehicles from France. They arrived and they settled there. The plan was that these huts would serve for 6 months. And the people will have by then moved to Auromodèle, and the huts would be given to the village. They are very close to the Kuilapalayam village, but things have gone differently, and the huts are still there and they are still inhabited by Aurovilians after 28 years *(Today, after more than 50 years, many of the huts are still standing and are still inhabited by Aurovilians).*

François Gautier

We left Paris on 15th August at zero hours *(midnight)*. Paris in August is totally empty. Everybody leaves Paris. It was a feeling of something being not dead, but like leaving an old world. I was 19, and I didn't know anything about India, but suddenly I understood I was leaving something behind me forever. There were old second- hand French cars, two old Citroen vans and two old Peugeots. There was a newer car driven by Papa Chenier. We worked on them in a garage in Paris for two months.

I was very young and didn't participate too much. The cars were not in good condition, and kept breaking down all the way from Paris to Auroville. They all made it here, but the vans broke down after Pakistan, and had to be towed by the two Peugeots from Pakistan or Afghanistan onwards. So we actually reached Auroville towing these two vans, which were out of order. The whole caravan was quite dramatic. We had accidents, and we had a lot of fights, people were very different, had different aspirations, different commitments to come here, and we were all very young. Except for people who had already come here and knew about Sri Aurobindo and Mother, like Vincenzo *(After having worked out the marble layering of the Urn for the inauguration of Auroville and coordinated the renovation work to create the Auroville Maternity in Promesse, Mother sent Vincenzo to France to put together the first caravan that drove to Auroville in 1969. He built the first Workshop of Auroville in Aspiration which Mother named, Toujours Mieux. Later it became known as Aureka. Vincenzo.passed away in 2012.)* and Stephen, an Australian who is not here anymore. There was Alain Monier and Eliane *(Alain and Eliane Monier left Auroville in the 80's and 90's respectively)* who knew a little about Sri Aurobindo and Mother.

The rest of us just had a faint idea of why we were coming. Not only were the cars in rather a bad state, but we all were a very motley group, and we were not united. I can't say it was a very harmonious or beautiful experience. There was a lot of conflict. On top of that, it was difficult because the caravan was not in good condition. We didn't have so much money, and there were the accidents. We got stuck in a place called Erzurum on the border between Turkey and Iran. It was terrible. We were stuck there for one week in the middle of nowhere. We stayed in a place that was very hot in the day and cold at night. We were attacked at night and had to protect our women. So it was kind of baffling. I came on the caravan without knowing anything about Auroville or Mother and Sri Aurobindo. I was never interested. Outwardly I didn't have the aspiration. I just felt that I wanted to get out of the life I had in France, as I had never been very happy there. Dimly and unconsciously I felt this is what I had to do, go out in the world and the caravan happened to be there, and I just took it by chance. As we progressed on the road from Paris to Auroville, I started reading Sri Aurobindo and Mother and Satprem's l'Aventure de la Conscience, which had just come out, and by the time I reached Delhi I knew this was it. I started without knowing where I was going, but by the time I reached Auroville, I knew I would stay all my life. So in a way it was very intense, but a very difficult experience.

Jean-Claude Bieri

I am a little bit optimistic, so for me, I remember much better the funny things than the very bad things. It was quite nice, quite funny. But it was difficult, because two tendencies were there for us very young people. The first one was to go very quickly to Auroville, and the other was to do a bit of sightseeing. But it was sure a lot of adventure, with breakdowns on the journey where there was no road, and we had a very bad piston. We had to repair the vehicle very often. It was funny to repair the vehicle at night without tools, without anything. It was a great adventure, like the pioneers in the far West of America at the beginning. I was playing. For me it was a great play all the time. I knew about Auroville from Bernard Delambre *(aka Janaka)*, who is still here, and he explained to me about Mother and Sri Aurobindo and the beginning of Auroville. I was interested but no more than that. What was interesting for me was the situation in France. It was becoming very difficult politically, and I was part of the 1968 movement in Paris. I was fighting against the police, and after that, I decided with Bernard to make a big travel experience around the world. I wanted to purchase a huge bus and to arrange a nice caravan to travel all around the world because France was dust for me. At that time Vincenzo came to France to start his own caravan for Auroville. Bernard was in contact with the Auroville Association. For me it was an opportunity to go with a group to India and maybe settle in Auroville, in a new city. I said, "why not, it could be interesting to be there for one year, and after that I will finish my trip." So I joined the caravan, and it was a very, very interesting experience, the trip from Europe to India. It was terrible somewhere, but so beautiful. For me it was…I cannot say a dream, but I had the opportunity to be in contact with so many different people, and to live together, and to fight with them. It was fantastic.

The big shock for me was arriving in Auroville. I thought the city was already started. I expected to see buildings, to see shops, to see roads and it was only bare land with nothing, no trees, nothing. That was a big shock. We were sitting in Aspiration in a few houses that were not even finished, and that was the beginning. So we had to start to work, and I started to work. We had to do it, so the only question we had for the architect at that time was what to do and how to do it. We had nothing but our bare hands to make everything. We only had the few tools we had brought with us. We had to repair our own vehicles, so we started to make a small workshop. The first thing we had to do was to finish the houses and make the first kindergarten. We had two kids, so we have to make a small school. That was the beginning. It was very difficult to imagine how to build a city when you don't know anything about it. I am not an architect or a plumber or an electrician. I learned everything in Auroville. That was a very great school, making practice when you're in school. We had no time to think about it, there was always something to do the next day and the next moment. I was working and that is all. Sometimes I tried to meditate also, but that was a little bit more difficult, and to read the books of Mother and Sri Aurobindo.

Sri Aurobindo was impossible to read, too complicated, because most of Sri Aurobindo was in English, and I didn't know English at all. What I learned in school was completely forgotten when I arrived in India, so I was not able to communicate with the people in English. So I started to relearn English. Like François, I was very impressed by Satprem's book, The Adventure of Consciousness. That was something very great. That may be what made me decide to stay here. We had to plant trees, we had to get water, and the kitchen was not ready. We had to build everything. There was no time to think.

Christophe Pitoeff

I had come to the Ashram to see my mother Svetlana, who had been here for some time. So I wrote to the Mother and said that I'd like to help, because I knew my brother was coming with the caravan.

That way I could help in Aspiration to prepare the huts to be finished. There was a lot of work to do. There was some painting and finishing touches, but it seems it was not quite ready, as Jean-Claude said. We did our best to get it ready on time.

A little while later another caravan arrived from Germany.

Dorothee Hach

I came a few months after the first French caravan had arrived here. How I came here was the coming together of many things, if I think about it. First, I had just finished my school. I should have gone to university then. Second, I met a group of people who just at that time came into contact with Sri Aurobindo. One fellow out of that group saw a photo of Sri Aurobindo in a bookshop which was on the cover of that first German book on Sri Aurobindo actually. It was a biography, which is still being published. He bought that book because he was so impressed with the photograph, and then we all read it and came together at the same time and we were all very much touched by it. After some time we came across an article about the inauguration of Auroville in '68, and we came to know this was the same thing - that this man, Sri Aurobindo, and Mother after him, had founded the city. We thought, "this is great, this is exactly what we want to do." After that we started to prepare our caravan. It was a little Volkswagen bus, which we built up for people to sleep inside. We were six people, three men and three ladies. There was a tent on top which could be flapped open, so three people could sleep up and three down. It was a nice trip. No one else from our group is here now. Problems started soon after we arrived. Our group was very different from the French group, which was already there. The other people couldn't adjust, and soon they started breaking away one after the other. I am the only one that is here now.

François

There were only a few palm trees. Everything was so red, and it was like snow in the morning and evening sun. It was gleaming, it was scintillating. There were no trees and you could see the sea everywhere. There was no road from the beach. We had to come via Jipmer Hospital and cross the village of Kuilapalayam. We built the road later in Aspiration. It was a shock. There were two worlds, our world and that of the village. There was so much gap.

Dorothee

Actually I remember when someone said that the problem with Aspiration was the proximity to the village - Mother said it was a major opportunity.

Christophe

We had frequent contact with the cows and the goats. That was the first encounter with the villagers. We had to fight against the goats to protect the few little trees here and there. They didn't understand our language sometimes, and we had to be firm.

Prem

The first meeting we had with the villagers in Kuilapalayam they threw stones at us. They were very upset, so I went to the Mother and told her that the main reason for this behaviour of the villagers was because we had not kept our promises.

You see, when the foundation took place, we brought water to that place. And then we said we'll give it to the villagers, and then we cut it off and it didn't go to the villages, so they were upset. So I said to

First public tap installed by Auroville in Kuilapalayam

Mother, "our major problem with the villages today is water." She said, "but there is plenty of water there." I said, "Mother, there is no water." Her response was, "no, my dear child, there is plenty of water, but it is underground." I said, "sorry, Mother, but the Government of Tamil Nadu has bored some wells, and they found no water in the ground." She said, "they're stupid, there is so much water, you can't imagine. You bring me the map." So we took the map of that area to her and she concentrated for a while and put her finger on one spot

and said, "you bore here." Gérard of AuroOrchard was arranging the manual boring in those days and we started drilling in that place. We went up to a certain depth and found no water. I went back to Mother and said, "Mother, there is no water." She said, "now listen, don't say that to me, you go further." So we went further, and within five meters or so we struck water. And that discovery of the Mother has changed the whole face of Auroville. The trees that you find now are because of that first borewell

that we put up, and it was absolutely a miracle. When the water flowed out of that particular well, you can't imagine the scene. All of us and three hundred villagers were dancing around that well.

G. Varadharajan

As a matter of fact I asked Mother whether I should work here. And she said yes, I can go and work in Kuilapalayam, because there was a very great necessity for the Tamil people to know what Auroville is about. Auroville is essentially a project expressing the inner spirit. If you want to concentrate on external things only for its own sake instead of as an expression of inner spirit, the main thrust of Auroville will be lost. The other things are there and they will happen, but as an expression of the spirit. I was 33 years. Even before that, since 1966, I was connected with Auroville. I was in Madras (now Chennai), and then the idea and the name was announced in 1964, so since 1966 I was connected with Auroville. I started staying in Auromodèle and Aspiration from 1969, January. Shyamala and I were the only Tamils, and we were cooking our own food, but we were living with the Westerners. It was a very nice experience and except for the cooking, all the other activities were with them.

Aspiration Cafeteria. Next to Piero (right) is Santosh, wife of Prem Malik

First workshop in Aspiration. Vincenzo (right) and Bhagavandas

We used to mix with them. First predominantly French and then slowly other nationalities came. There was always an interaction, and we were a small community of about 30 or 40 people, and all knew each other, so it was interesting. They came in 1969, you know the young people in their 20's. They were as brilliant, or as turbulent, or as enthusiastic, as has been reported. So it was a very good experience for me. One thing about them was they had tremendous goodwill for Auroville. These people were young and their life was moving very fast, so far as the villages were concerned, as their life was moving very slow. Naturally there was an adjustment, so problems used to come. It was all settled amicably by means of talk, and naturally, when people here came to know these Westerners meant well in their hearts, they could catch the vibrations, so that solved the problem - not because of their high benefits, or whatever they received from them, but because they knew in their hearts that they were meaning well, so that saved all the situations.

Govindaraj from Kuilapalayam

First Mother was purchasing the lands, and these Westerners had come. I was thinking these Westerners may drive all the local people away, but they did some social work for essential things. They gave water and medical facilities, so in the course of time everything became alright. They did a lot of afforestation and there was a lot of interaction between the people and mutual goodwill and confidence developed. It was alright except for some minor things. They started schools also, so our children were studying there, so we were all happy about it. *(translated from Tamil by Varadharajan)*

Poonga from Kuilapalayam

I am 66, so you can guess how old I was then. There were between 1500 and 2000 people in Kuilapalayam then. We were afraid that these *velakaras*, I mean Westerners, might do some harm. They might lift *(kidnap)* the children or they may convert them to some other religion or take them to their country. *(translated from Tamil by Varadharajan)*

Meeting the Mother

Most early Aurovilians met the Mother. She gave four public Darshans a year, which nearly all Aurovilians went to. Also most went to see her on their birthdays. Some saw her more often, and several people from Aspiration had the privilege of meeting her every week over a period of a few months.

Danielle

Somebody told me about Auroville in '67 in London, so I read a little booklet and I felt it was the place I wanted to live in. Then I came, and there was the experience with Mother, so actually the contact with Mother was the most important thing in the beginning. It was a very intimate contact which changes your life, and I was always feeling her with me. It was the most important thing, even before Auroville, I would say.

Dhandapani

One day Rod *(Rod Hemsell presently lives in USA and visits Auroville regularly)* told me that we were going to see the Mother, so then I went with him to see her. We waited and then we went inside, and we both had Darshan. We walked in, so beautiful inside, a nice and clean room with beautiful flowers. Mother had lots of presents, beautiful embroidered cloth and nice chairs. It was really wonderful to go in that room, and I felt very, very happy. She was putting some force into me, or clearing something, but I felt it was a wonderful experience. When we came out, she gave us a blessings packet, and a rose. It was a small packet, and I still have lots of them with me.

Francis

Basically we feel that we are all being guided by the Mother. We were guided by the Mother then, and we are being guided by the Mother now. And basically that is why we are here. It was quite tangible in the first five years of Auroville, because she was in her body, and you could go and see her, and you could ask her questions. Sometimes we would get answers, and sometimes we wouldn't, but the guidance is definitely continuous.

Jocelyn

I wrote Mother and I said, "Mother, what should I do?" And Mother said, "find your psychic being. Try and I will help you." In those days people actually were walking around saying, "did you hear that Mother said that nature has confirmed that the supramental transformation can happen." People were really excited about the spiritual objectives of Sri Aurobindo's yoga. It was an incredible place. This was the new world.

Michael Z

I was reliving this bicycle ride around Auroville, and seeing this parched, dry, eroded, barren landscape that I had bicycled through all day, and as I contemplated this arid, dry, hot dusty landscape in my heart, it started to rain, and it was like this unbelievably sweet rainfall in my heart, and it was Mother's Grace. And I wrote and told her about the experience, and she sent a blessings packet and a letter saying "yes, welcome" and that was it. I never went to Japan. In fact, I hardly left Pondicherry for the next ten years.

Gloria

Auroville was just a barren land on which all our dreams were projected, so there was a lot of expectation. For me the strongest memory was the physical presence of the Mother. The contact with her was so overwhelming, and so full of hope, and so full of marvelous things, that all the rest was just an adventure. After having seen a few children born, because there was a maternity clinic in Promesse where we lived, the 5 year old daughter we brought with us asked continuously for a sister or brother. She wanted a small child in the house. It was very beautiful to offer to Mother a new inhabitant for Auroville, a new Aurovilian, so we decided to have a second child. It was really a very, very beautiful experience, because going to see Mother with her physical presence, it was something like the soul of the child was coming through her, even the presence of the child was so much felt before the birth. And so it was very intense.

Prem

I arrived in Pondicherry at a time when Auroville was non-existent, you could say. It was just there as a thought, but not in reality because the foundation took place later on. And I was asked by the Mother to work for Auroville. That is how I came into contact with the whole thing. Otherwise from my own part, it was not a movement to Auroville. It was a movement to Mother and Sri Aurobindo, and I came to Pondicherry for that. Then the Mother said, "no, you are to work for Auroville."

Ananda

I joined the Ashram in 1958, when I was eleven years old, and since then, of course, I knew the Mother. But knowing her then, and knowing her now, are quite different, because at the time I came to Auroville, I was a young lad of 22 going through my education. At that time, I should say, I knew the Mother more theoretically. I knew she was the divine Mother, as we were told. We read about that, but the inner contact was only to the level of the heart. That means, yes, we loved the Mother, but today I can say the contact is much deeper. It is beyond the level of the heart; there is a deeper experience, surely.

Bhaga Gabriau

One of my students in Paris had a book in his hand and he told me to look, as he had found something which seemed quite interesting. I looked, and it was the Life Divine by a certain Sri Aurobindo. I had never seen that name anywhere before, and I still remember, I was standing there at the door of my room, and I read the first four pages. All of a sudden it was as if from the entire universe billions of pieces of a huge puzzle assembled in front of me.

There was the most magnificent vision of the future of the earth, of the future of humanity, of the meaning and purpose of life, and that was so unalterably wonderful, my whole being gave itself to that at that minute. I sat down and I said to God, "okay, that's really worth living." That's how I became interested in this yoga.

Charlie Lammert

How Mother spoke about Auroville, what it was to be an Aurovilian, and the purpose of Auroville, was enough to inspire me.

Christophe

On the very last day, or just two days before leaving Pondicherry to start teaching in the south of France, I went to see Mother and said to her very simply, "Mother, I just don't feel like going. I feel this is my home, this is my place." Mother said, "you can stay here as long as you like." And I'm still here. With Mother, everything was absolutely so simple, so straightforward.

François

If one remembers something from the Mother, it was her eyes. The magnet that drew you was her eyes, and that first time I just froze. I cannot describe what happened. I don't really remember, but I just froze and I didn't know where I was.

Christophe

What I remember most about Mother, after the eyes, was the strength of her hands. I was absolutely amazed, when she wanted to convey something she had such strength in her hands, yes, physical strength. Absolutely unbelievable when she was holding your hands; it was really an experience. Of course there was something else behind, but she was really trying to materialize something so very, very strongly and deeply.

Dorothee

It was just as Cristophe said, things completely disappeared. I was exactly like Cristophe after my first meeting with Mother on my birthday. I had to be guided out. I didn't know the way at all, or where I was. I stayed in the meditation room afterwards downstairs, and it took me a long time to come back.

Joss Brooks

In those early years there was the vision of the Mother, and she communicated that to us strongly. We were these spaced out refugees from the 60's, but that vision of an incredible, subtle, supple place was a vision that you could see. It was tangible then. You sat in the middle of these empty fields and you looked. I know that was my case. You looked for long enough and you could see what was going to be, whether it was colour, or whether it was form. This incredible, subtle garden... and that is what she told us, told me. It wasn't just afforestation, go out and plant a whole lot of trees. No. It was something else that she was giving you a picture of and slowly we saw that, like those colouring books that you put water on and the pictures come up. We were putting water on, and this picture was emerging. Now to me the excitement is that vision is coming into reality, and it will get more and more detail.

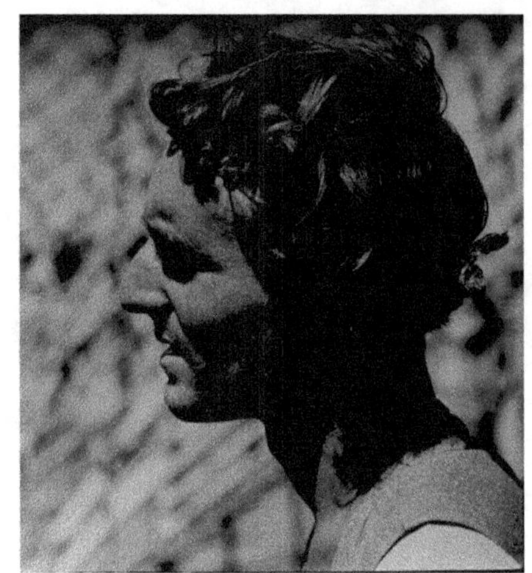

Aster Patel

My experience didn't begin with Auroville. It began with Sri Aurobindo and the Mother, and Auroville came into it at a later stage. I came with my parents to the Ashram, and to Sri Aurobindo and the Mother in 1943. There was a group of around 300 adults around Sri Aurobindo and the Mother and no children, so it was quite a situation, and the Mother said to my parents, "you come here with your children." I was nine, my brother was five. But the moment two of us as children were there, the Mother set herself the task of taking full care of the children. When we met her three or four times a day, we had occasion to take everything to her. To have grown up in an atmosphere of that charge is something that does not leave one's being ever after. And the four occasions in the year when one had the *Darshan* of Sri Aurobindo was an experience that, even as a child, lives with you perhaps for lives to come.

I studied philosophy and psychology at the Centre of Education. In my early 20's, when I finished the course, something which had always been with me began to surface, which was to have the other half of one's inheritance, to know the thought and culture of the Western world. I chose Paris, not any other place, Paris and the Sorbonne and with a very specific clear purpose - to study European thought and culture, to study the new ideas that were around in Europe at the time, and to read again Sri Aurobindo in the context of European thought and culture. So I took up the work of a PhD thesis at the Sorbonne on Sri Aurobindo's work and that of a French philosopher. They were very intense years for me, years of learning, of synthesizing, of harmonizing all the time. I used to come home very often, every year. That was a necessity, and from there to write to the Mother how the ideas and thoughts were taking shape. She would write, she would talk, she would advise, "see this." She gave a shape to the whole process that was going on.

My first indication for the Auroville experience, which had started when I was not here, although I had heard about it, was a letter I received from the Mother early in 1970. I was just finishing my work, packing up and ready to get back home to the Ashram. She said that the United Nations in New York was observing its 25th anniversary, and for that they were having a World Youth Assembly, and they were having delegations of young people from around the world. Each country was sending a delegation. Now the youngsters were going to talk about their ideas of what they thought the future of man ought to be. How should the future evolution take place in different areas, be it in politics, in economics, in education, in culture, in social organization, etc. And the letter said that Mother wanted me to be part of the Indian delegation, and that I should proceed to New York for that.

Chapter 3, 1970

The Aspiration Talks

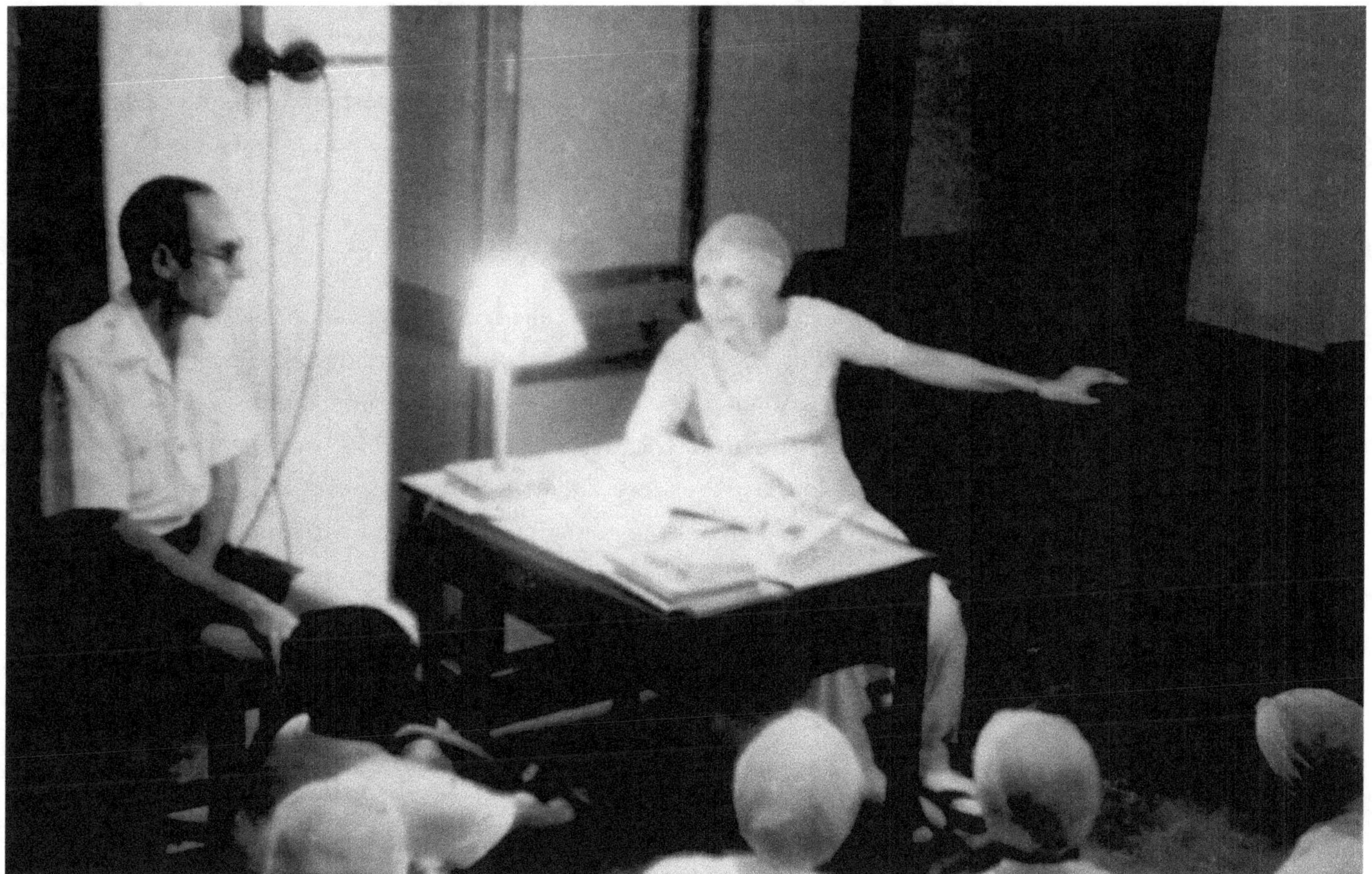

In Mother's room

Several of the early residents of Aspiration would visit the Mother in her room every one or two weeks. These came to be known as the Aspiration Talks. One of the things she talked with them about was the true spirit of Auroville, and what it meant to be a true Aurovilian.

Varadharajan

I was in Auroville even before the first group of Westerners came to Aspiration. It was a very interesting group. I was staying in Aspiration when there was a unique opportunity of being guided by the Mother. At that time we could go to the Mother once in two weeks in a group of people. So that gave a certain fundamental grounding upon which to start our life in Auroville. We were very much committed to live a community life.

Christophe

What I can say about these Aspiration Talks, as they've now been called, is that we felt in the beginning to really build the city we had to build something within us. And we had this conflict of being asked to build something concretely, to build a city, to have factories, and all these things. At the same time there was this aspiration, this urge... We were reading Satprem, and a little bit of Mother and Sri Aurobindo, and we felt that the inner discovery had to be made. But how do we do that? We were like little children on the way. We felt very much the need of asking the Mother whether she could give some guidance and see us from time to time. So I wrote to her and got the reply that she was willing to see us once a week. I don't remember if she immediately said once a week. She said "come and see me on Tuesday." So we went and saw her, with Bhagavandas (still living in Auroville) and Alain Monier, on Tuesday. When we would arrive, there used to be an exchange of flowers with her. We would bring some flowers from Aspiration, and she would give back some flowers that she was keeping on her lap or on the table next to her. I remember once we brought to her some service flowers, a big bunch of these yellow flowers. The people around were a little uneasy, because she had this big bunch of flowers on her, but she was smiling, she was so happy. And after that she gave four flowers of transformation to each of us, and she said, "service leads to transformation", a hint that to serve, you have to work, to give yourself. At the end of each of these entretiens (talks) with the Mother, she would say "au revoir" and take our hands in hers.

Actually, very soon she asked us whether we wanted to ask questions or whether we would rather have what she called a "bath of silence." Usually we said we'd rather have a bath of silence. For about 15 or 20 minutes we would just stay in front of her in "silence", I mean silence in quotes. Once she said after the meditation, "a very noisy silence." We were quite a number of us there. After that she said "other people can come if they are sincere and if they want to come, if it helps, if they find it's good for them." So sometimes we were about 15 or 20 in this little room full of green and gold. This green carpet and the golden light from the windows, and

Mother there in the golden and the green. It was really an unforgettable experience. All of us there trying very hard to meditate, to concentrate - in front of her we had to be good. You would go and see the Mother and you would expect something, you were a bit scared in the beginning, you thought, "oh, so simple and so Mother-like and so humorous", and she said, "oh, a very noisy silence, un silence bruyant."

Dorothee

I contributed my share of noise to the silence. I can't say very much. First, it was surprising to me because she very much insisted that we should be very comfortable. Several times she would repeat that we must be comfortable, and we would try moving around, and afterwards there was a noisy silence.

Jean-Claude

My experience! I remember I was a little bit afraid somewhere, because I was a part of this very noisy silence. I knew very well and I remember somewhere inside something was saying, "shut up, shut up, you must be concentrating more and be more open. Open yourself, open yourself. You come here to be open." And I was adding more to the noisy silence. I was very, very uncomfortable, because Mother was so immense compared to me. I felt so little and so unprepared for what she was asking us to do. I remember that.

Christophe

She could immediately feel if you had some ideas in your head, and she would say, "Oh I can feel those ideas, the head is full of ideas, but ideas are not very good." That was one thing that we understood, that to build Auroville, we should not have too many ideas. It should come in a different way. That was one very practical piece of advice she gave us.

Jean-Claude

She was guiding us, yes obviously, but I don't remember she gave us any counsel or advice about what we had to do for gaining consciousness. She smiled always. It was very simple for her. "You have to work, to try and be as conscious as possible in the work you are doing." That was the advice she gave. Other advice I don't remember.

Christophe

We had gone to her with many questions in our heads. And in front of her, the experience that we had so many times was that questions disappeared, in the sense that she threw the light on the problem, and we were left sitting there, and wondering "what was my problem? What was the question I wanted to ask?" That was a wonderful experience that everything was just as it should have been. She immediately put you in contact with what was really true, your true self, your true being. And for a short while in front of her, you really had no problem at all. But I remember the very first question. I was trying to remember, remember, yes I had come with a question. I should put at least one question. I asked about the work, as that was the most important thing for us, about the work in Aspiration, how to proceed. She immediately felt there was the tendency to escape a little bit from the work that had to be done. And she said that the inner discovery should have been done before coming to Auroville.

This was the very, very striking thing she said, that it would have been much better and much easier. But of course it was not always the case for us. She stressed the importance of the very, very physical work. She gave us some so wonderful details. I mean you can do anything with this attitude of trying to find the true attitude, just cycling, and just planting a tree, just doing anything, sweeping, cooking. It was so wonderful, this very first talk with her, when she stressed that just with physical work you could have communion with the Divine. It was very important for us, because we had this tendency of thinking that everything can be done by a miracle. I mean we were very young and thought that maybe there was another way of building the city, not just building factories and producing all these things that we were told to do. But she made it clear that we have to find the Divine here on this Earth through physically working and finding the true attitude.

After some time, during all these talks we had with her on every Tuesday, she told us that she would very much like to try and find with us the true spirit of Auroville, what a true Aurovilian should be. This was how it started, with the help of Satprem, because after our meeting with the Mother, she would meet with Satprem also, and each time she would ask us what we thought, what would be the most important thing to be a true Aurovilian.

So in the beginning each one of us would say this and that, and little by little, she made a sort of a chart. It is known now as "To Be a True Aurovilian," the first few points. She had intended to continue, but for some reason that we never came to know, she interrupted those talks after a few months and we were left to ourselves.

To Be A True Aurovilian

1. The first necessity is the inner discovery by which one learns who one really is behind the social, moral, cultural, racial and hereditary appearances. At our inmost centre there is a free being, wide and knowing, who awaits our discovery and who ought to become the acting centre of our being and our life in Auroville.

2. One lives in Auroville in order to be free of moral and social conventions; but this liberty must not be a new slavery to the ego, its desires and its ambitions. The fulfillment of desires bars the route to the inner discovery which can only be attained in peace and the transparency of a perfect disinterestedness.

The First School

One of the first tasks facing the people of Aspiration was the education of the children. One child had come with them on the caravan, another was born shortly after the caravan arrived, and there were a few children in other parts of Auroville who had been brought here by their parents. There were also several children from the villages who were by now closely involved with the early Aurovilians. So a school started in Aspiration towards the end of 1970. Many of the students at that school are still in Auroville today.

Dhandapani (in the front)

Sports, Ananda

Eliane Monier serves lunch

Selvaraj (center) and friends

Dhandapani

When I started living in Forecomers, I didn't know how to read and write English or Tamil. I didn't go to any village school. Bob and Deborah were trying to tell me something about reading or writing, or learning to speak English or other languages, so they said that I have to go to school. Before going to school, I was also doing messenger work. I learned to ride Deborah's bicycle. It was very big. She was a tall woman, and the cycle was so high. I would fall many times, because I couldn't reach the seat. So I would hold the handlebar and take a chit, and come to Centre Field sometimes, or to Centre Kitchen, to give some messages.

I used to just hold the handle and put my weight on both sides and try to pedal all the way up and down, and I had a very good experience learning how to ride a cycle.

Then they brought me one day to this place in Centre Field, where there were one or two capsules at that time and beautiful jackfruit trees. Rod was there, but I don't remember where he was living. He was all the time playing his flute. I used to come and sit in this capsule with a round table in the middle. Rod was my first teacher. But this man was new to me, so I took a very long time to look at his face. I learned to do paintings with him. And he was teaching me English, so I was trying to put some letters on the paper, which I saw for the first time. I saw wonderful colours, which I tried to use with the brush. And after trying and trying, I managed to draw a donkey.

At first there was not really a fixed school in Auroville, as there were not enough children. Then they started school in Aspiration. They started Kindergarten and small schools there. After that, my brother and another brother joined me at Forecomers, and from there we would walk all the way to Aspiration across the fields, just open fields. Sometimes you would have a field of peanuts and we would walk across.

Everything we did was new, was something which we hadn't seen before in our lives. Even the *chappals*, which Bob and Deborah brought for us, were new. When we would walk into the village, we had about 10-15 children around us, just looking at our yellow *chappals*, because they didn't even have that. And our tennis shoes were a very great thing. It was wonderful. The whole of life was just moving so fast, with these wonderful new things which happened.

Poonga

My children were there, and people found me honest, and they asked me to come to the mother and child care centre, and then I went to work in the kindergarten. I went to one French lady who was running a kindergarten, who wanted someone who was decent and honest. There were about twenty Tamil children going to Eliane's school, including my four children: Mani, Shiva, Rajaveni, Shivagami. My children were doing very well in Auroville. *(translated from Tamil by Varadharajan)*

Alok Aurovillian

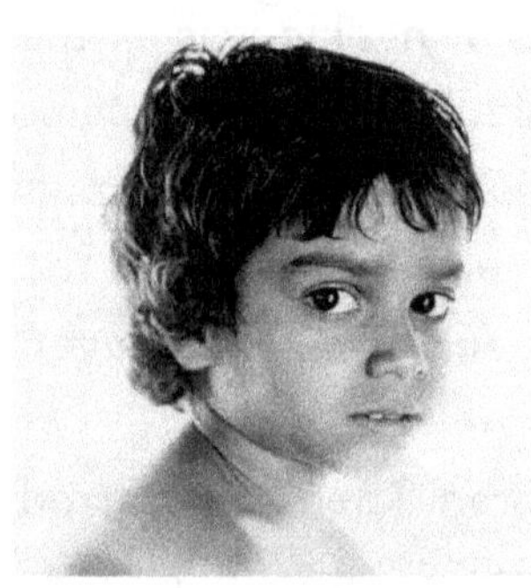

I went to the French kindergarten that Alain and Eliane had started, and I learned to read and write in French. That was my first language. I was speaking Hindi at home, and I would go to school and learn French. It was a little confusing at first, because my other friends would speak Tamil, so I was picking up Tamil as well. But the kindergarten had a very structured environment, where we had to sit properly, eat properly, and wash our hands. Everything was done just right. There was a lot of discipline there, but other than that, what I really enjoyed from growing up here was that we had to be very creative in our games, because we didn't have toys. I still remember how we would play all types of games with sticks and stones and trees, and there was just no need to have or buy something from somewhere else in order to have fun, so I think we just had to be very resourceful and creative.

None of my educational experience compares to that kindergarten stage. There were just so many things that we did and learned.

D. Selvaraj

I thought that I would become a painter one day. The painting is still there in my memory and there was a lot of playing, and crafts, and going to the beach. We used to go to Far Beach *(now Sri Ma)* and do wall painting. I don't remember doing much writing and reading and things. Maybe at a later stage we did that.

R. Ravi

I still remember my vision of the school was something which I don't find nowadays. It was a very wonderful time for me in terms of conditions and studies with the teachers. I always think of the past, but I never think of what happened. The past one can never find nowadays. Those were the wonderful days with the collective, the teachers, the students, and the games. Those days were my special days.

Savitra Lithman

I remember meeting an Australian guy and asking him what is Auroville, and he fumbled around trying to tell me, and then asked me to come out to Auroville with him. I remember bicycling out with him, and he took me along this road that turns off by the watchtower, and you come out along the beach road, and suddenly we were in this no-man's-land, cows and goats, and absolutely nothing else, and no more road. We got these bicycles, and I am still coming out of a Western orientation, and I was beginning to really question what I was getting myself into. Then we hit these canyons, and I remember we had to take the bicycles and carry them, and I came into what turned out to be the back end of Forecomers.

The first people I met were Deborah and Bob, an American couple, who were two of the early pioneers, and they were about as far out an example of early Aurovilians as you could get. Bob was in a loin cloth and Deborah was in a long flowing robe. They invited me to tea. They served algae biscuits. Bob was cultivating algae. The more I tried to understand, the more things seemed running faster and out of control to me. But I found some kind of strange 'at-homeness' in this insanity.

So when I got back to Pondicherry that night, I decided to write and ask Mother if I could stay and work in Auroville. A few days later she said I could start working in the school. This was when I got involved with Auroville, after having spent the first six or eight months in Pondicherry.

The school was meant to start on December 15 of 1970, so there was this frantic six weeks of getting everything together. I remember there was a shed, which used to be a kind of workshop-garage, and we were meant to turn this thing into a school. So that's how I came tumbling into the story.

Ananda

In 1969, I had completed my higher course - that is, the education at the Ashram. Then I went to the Mother, asking her what work I should take up and she gave me the choice. She said, "you can be in the Ashram or in Auroville. It is your choice." Therefore I did come out to Auroville to look around and see for myself what exactly is Auroville. Since the inauguration in '68, two years had passed, and I wanted to see how it was all coming about. Then I was convinced of this sense of collaboration, unity, and friendship, and I went back to Mother in 1970 on my birthday, and she asked me what my decision was. I said, "Mother, I would like to go to Auroville." She concentrated for a while and she said, "très bien, that is a good choice." And when I asked her what work I should take up, she said very interestingly, "do you know André?"

André was Mother's son. I said, "oui, douce Mère." She said, "go to André and he will tell you what to do." And so from there I went straight to André and I told him that Mother had sent me to him. So there in the beginning André said, "you be a link between the Ashram and the Auroville administration." That's how I came into Auroville.

Later on, Mother asked Norman Dowsett *(who taught at Ashram School and helped to set up the first school in Aspiration. He passed away many years ago.)* to take me into the school, and I became in charge of the school in Aspiration. I still remember the day I walked into Aspiration. It was 1971, 1st of January, it was in the afternoon. I have taken a calendar from the Mother and the calendar's message was, "Blessed are those who take a leap towards the future." It was so symbolic for me that I was taking a leap into the future. I really walked from Pondicherry down to Aspiration with a calendar, and I said I'm going towards my future.

Shraddhavan Stuttle

If we go back to the opening day, Mother's son, Monsieur André Morisset, was sent to open Aspiration School. As far as I remember, the message that Mother gave was "a sincere will to know and to progress." At the same time she had been asked what languages are going to be used in Auroville schools, and it is interesting that at a much earlier date in '65 or so, she had said predominantly Tamil. I only came to know that recently. But at the time when the school opened, on December 16, 1970, then she distinctly gave Tamil first as the local language, then English as the international language, French - she didn't give an explanation -, and simplified Sanskrit as the future language of India.

So we tried from the very beginning, even when things were so formless, that at least something should be happening in each of these four languages. I remember my first Sanskrit lesson. It was so moving to me. I felt this is really the language of my soul, these first simple chantings that we did. I think she taught us 'Gachami', something that had 'gachami,' meaning, "I take refuge."

Savitra

I was totally unprepared, in the sense that as I was a very introverted kind of guy, very into books, and an internal orientation with my life, and these kids pulled me out. They forced me to become who I was, despite the fact that I would have much preferred, by my orientation, to have stayed internalized. That was not at all my nature. However, it was that in writing to Mother and asking for work that I wound up being given the work in Aspiration School. It turned out to be the way that I was born into my Auroville experience, and made me a totally other person from the kind of guy I probably would have been. That thread of children stays through everything I've done ever since then.

Shraddhavan

If you look at the personality building aspect, I think that for all of us it was just marvellous, just incredible. It had something to do with there being no artificial props. You really only had your personal relationship between you and the kids. And that had to be absolutely honest with the surrounding circumstances. That gave us an experience, a growing experience, and a certain trust was built up among all of us. As Alok said, it was this kind of resourcefulness, and what Ange mentioned to me the other day, when she said that the aspiration to do something really super was so living among everybody, kids and adults.

Yes, I have to admit that there were a lot of shortcomings, organizational shortcomings from the point of view of communicating skills, things that young people should know and should have access to. But on the other hand, all of us shared an experience that many people never get in their lives, and we should be very, very grateful for that. I don't know if you can imagine, but we only had a bare *keeth* shed with bamboo walls. The floor had been nicely painted and it had a new keeth roof. There was no furniture. There was no equipment. There was nothing. Somebody donated some of the beds that were issued to Aurovilians in those days. If you came to live in Aspiration, you would get a place to live and you would get a bed. If you were lucky, you would get a table and a chair as well, but basically you got a bed and a mattress. We could sit on the floor, and use the beds as tables. For these 35 kids, perhaps we had three beds. And the person who was nominally in charge of the school was Norman Dowsett, an educationist from the Ashram in Pondicherry, and he was friendly with the manager of the Handmade Paper Factory in Pondicherry. He had donated huge stacks of sheets of beautifully coloured handmade paper. So we had this paper and some pairs of scissors, which lasted about three days, not more. And that was how we had to start.

Savitra

Shraddhavan was living in Auroville when the school began and I was living in Pondicherry, so I used to come out on the bus with the Pondicherry kids and some of the adults. The teachers on the bus were all North Indians except for me. The first day that we actually had school was when all the preconceptions I had experienced about going into an educational thing, about the Auroville of the future, fell right before my feet, along with my expectations. Because here we had this group of kids, several dozen children from all these different cultures, none of whom spoke the same language, except maybe a handful. There were Italians, and there were French, there were North and South Indians, and there were German kids, and a few who spoke English, and for any of us who had ideas about what we were going to do, we didn't even have a basic language to start with. And I remember there were these bricks inside this garage that had been converted into a school thing, and we wound up building them into a boat. Making a boat from these bricks was the first exercise that we did with the children. Somehow that brick boat floated.

Shraddhavan

I mean the first months were chaos, sometimes alarming chaos, but what gradually got established was some very genuine kind of relationship between everyone. We couldn't impose anything on these kids, so if we wanted them to be with us, to absorb anything from us, we had to be with them. And I remember spending hours playing Ludo *(a strategy board game)* with some of these little kids, because this way you can learn to count, you could learn the names of the colours, and you can develop some kind of social skills.

Savitra

Art was the medium of language, since it was impossible to work with some kind of mental framework. The children could relate to you drawing. I remember endlessly drawing flowers, until I was sick of drawing flowers. But they would keep asking, and eventually you could start to work out from what you were drawing, and drawing with them, and identifying and getting language names for the things you were drawing, and slowly it worked out. Art was the common language in the beginning, and also physical activities. We used to take them to the beach. I remember we used to walk through the canyons, and there was a lot of adventure time. The adults, the teachers used to meet together in the evenings very often. We would have frantic sessions about how to make the school work, and rarely did it correspond to any of the things we were talking about. It just had to work itself out, and have its own sense, and the kids primarily were the determining factor.

Shraddhavan

Going to the beach was like crossing the Sahara. Now it looks so green between Aspiration and the beach, and we had to run because we didn't have chappals even, and the sand was so hot. These things we remember.

Many of the children who attended school in Aspiration lived in Pondicherry. Each day they would come to Aspiration by bus. Then the bus would make a trip around Auroville to all the existing communities transporting people and things.

Ravi

We had a very wonderful day with our school bus, as most of the students used to come from Pondicherry to Aspiration by bus. It came by 8:00 to Aspiration and dropped off all the teachers and children. It then went back to Pondicherry, and whoever wanted to go to Pondicherry could go on the same bus. It came back to Auroville by 11:30, by lunch time. It then went back to Pondicherry, returned by 4:30 to pick up all the children and teachers going to Pondicherry. This transport was very good for us. People would stay in Aspiration because in those days we never had any transport, except cycling. If we wanted to see films we went to the Ashram Playground. Alok, me, Savitra and other people used to go along with this bus to the Ashram, where we had our meals, and we saw films, especially children's films.

We didn't see films for adults. We were given rooms where we could stay overnight and go to the *Samadhi*. Next day morning we could come back on the same bus. This transport service was a wonderful transport for all of us who used to stay in Aspiration. It used to come to Matrimandir also. This was a routine trip. Aspiration, Matrimandir, Moratandi, and back to Pondicherry.

Shraddhavan

Loaded up with stuff everyone did their shopping, piled up into the bus. It would be dropping off people and things.

Alok

That's why it was possible to live in far out communities in Auroville, because we had this bus coming through every day. So when we were living in Hope for about six months, we had to catch that bus every morning to come down to Aspiration, and it became very difficult after a time, because if we missed the bus, we had to walk all the way down across Auroville. There were people who had moved to Aurogarage *(situated on the main road to Pondicherry and no longer part of Auroville)* and, Promesse from Aspiration, just because they needed new settlers in those areas, and it was possible to live there and still be a part of the community, because of this transport. At that time I guess you didn't have a choice about where you were going to live. When you joined

Auroville, if the only place that was available was out there at Aurogarage, or Promesse, you had to go out and live there, so this bus service is something that I remember because we used it a lot.

Savitra

I remember the horn, whampwhamp eh whampwhamp.

Lisbeth Nusselein

We were staying in an Ashram Guesthouse in Pondicherry, when work in the new nursery and on the Matrimandir was going to start, and there was this new blue bus that was going to Auroville. After breakfast, which we had in the Ashram Dining Room every day, we took this bus which left from the park and went to Auroville to work.

Shraddhavan

We had a driver called Louis Swamy. He was a real tough fellow, and he had to be, because the 'Tibetan Army' used to come out every day from Pondicherry.

Savitra

She means the Tibetan children.

Shraddhavan

You know there was this lovely idea from a Tibetan student who had studied in the Ashram School when Auroville started. He felt there are so many homeless Tibetan children all over India, and if some of those young children could come and grow up in Auroville, they would manifest the Tibetan Pavilion. And he proposed this idea to the Mother and to the Dalai Lama, and both of them liked that idea, so the Tibetan government actually sanctioned for thirty children. But first ten came, and then we got a couple more. The maximum number we ever had was twelve, and they came in a big bunch in the second year of the school, with two lamas to look after them. But as there was no place for them in Auroville, they stayed in a house on Canteen Street in Pondicherry that was being used as a Tibetan carpet factory.

It's incredible to think these kids were just taken away from their families. The youngest was five or six at the time. Tashi *(she still lives in Auroville)* was seven. The oldest boy was twelve. They were just taken away from

Tashi with lama teacher

wherever they were, and dumped down here. They had an incredible solidarity. And they used to come out fighting on the bus in the morning. They would arrive fighting, and they would fight their way through the day, until about three o'clock in the afternoon, and by then everybody else would be absolutely exhausted, and then they would bring their books and say, "shouldn't we learn to read now." Then you could, maybe for an hour, do something with them. So we found this situation very, very difficult. There was one Englishman, Derek *(no longer in Auroville)*, who took them as his special responsibility and he did a wonderful job with them. But we wanted them to come and live in Auroville. We felt they are so disturbed, because of this carpet factory business, that if we could distribute them in families, this would be so much better. We found the families, and everyone would be willing to take one or two Tibetan children, and the idea was put to Mother, but she was absolutely clear. She said, "no, they are here to represent Tibet and their culture and they must stay together until you can provide a boarding where they can all live together." It was on that occasion that she said that the only unity worth having is the Divine Unity that can embrace all differences.

Regarding where we thought the school was going, Mother had given these names for the schools. There were supposed to be seven buildings, and she was asked what are they to be called, so she gave the names "Last School, After School 1, 2 & 3, Super School, and No School." It was a kind of challenge to us, to understand what she meant by that. If this is Last School, where are we going? We had a dream that at least for some of the children and for some of the adults it would be possible to have a kind of 24 hour education, where we would live together, and just be learning together all the time.

The "Tibetan army"

So there was a move in that direction. Another thing we were really trying to do was based on the idea that No School would mean that the whole of Auroville would be the school, that there is no separate educational environment. So I think it was in 1972, when we had a period of months when the children went out every day to some community in ones and twos, and Shanti *(no longer in Auroville)* and I were trying to organize who could go where. It was quite strenuous, and finally we couldn't keep it up. For example we would send the kids all the way to Utility and then discover Mali's cow was sick, so he had to go to the vet, and these kinds of things. *(There were very few telephones in Auroville, so it was difficult to send messages.)* Gerhard was building a boat at what is now Sri Ma, and we used to send kids all the way down there. That attempt, that dream was there that all the production units, all the activities would somehow welcome the children in, and this would be somehow part of the education process. So these were two of the things we dreamed of. But at the same time there was the idea that these After School places would be very, very rich resource centres in different areas. Shanti's area was science, there was the library, and then there'd be other possibilities, such as theatre. A lot of people were interested in the performing arts, dance and so on.

Savitra

That concept continues through today though. It was part of the abstract ideas, which would go up and down, to find ways where the community became the educational environment, including the workshops and the garages. At Toujours Mieux *(a metal workshop now called Aureka)*, I remember there was an attempt with Jean *(Jean Pougault, a founding member of Toujours Mieux, is still living in Auroville)*. It would last for a moment, and even in the community the idea was accepted, and then it would fail. It would fall back into the school as school, and when I say to this day this tension goes on, it is because I can see how the community as a whole, as a collective, continues to struggle with what priority it gives to the children.

Chapter 4, 1971

Heidi and Patrick in Fertile

Building a capsule

Afforestation, Farming, and Community Building

As more people came, new settlements like Kottakarai, Forecomers and Fertile, started in the area which was to become the greenbelt. Other early communities were Utility and Fraternity, near the village of Kuilapalayam.

1971 was the year when many of the people who would later dedicate themselves to restoring and preserving a natural habitat arrived. As well as planting trees, they grew food and their first teachers were the villagers, who depended on agriculture for survival.

Joss (left)

Francis planting seedlings

Charlie

I came here at the end of 1971 and stayed in Pondicherry for a few months. I came to Auroville quite frequently, almost daily, but I wasn't living here. I would go and visit a community on the beach. Actually during the first few months I didn't go to Forecomers, where I wound up living eventually. I would come out towards the Matrimandir Nursery, which was just at the very beginning at that time. Nobody was there. It was all plants and pots. Then there were two people who were staying in Forecomers, and they wanted to go on a holiday for a week or so, so they said I could use their house. It was a floor and a keeth roof. There were no walls or anything. So I went out there, and it turned out that these people decided never to return, so I found myself living there in Forecomers, without anyone like Francis even knowing that I had moved in. One day I was going by, and Francis called out and said, "hello I see you going back and forth here, what are you doing?" And I said, "I live here." That was actually in the area where Success, the tree nursery, got set up later. At that time it was not a separate place. It was all Forecomers.

In the beginning, I was a tambi and Francis was in charge, and I would do whatever he said, work out in the fields, or help to dig the pits. A lot of times I did nothing, just hung out. By the time I got to Forecomers, my money was almost gone, but in those days that was not a problem. In those days one could live in Auroville with no money. Those who had took care of you. You just showed up in the kitchen and ate. There was no difficulty.

Jaap den Hollander

I came in the beginning of '71 *(Jaap arrived with Lisbeth Nusselein)*. We stayed the first couple of months in Pondicherry in a guest-house and came out to Auroville every day by bus, because there was no place to live in Auroville. So we hung out in Pondicherry for two or three months, and at some point a hut became available in a community called Silence, where Bharat Nivas is now built. So I moved in there for a while and stayed until Silence was removed

from the place, because it wasn't in the city plan. Silence, in those days, was known as the slums of Auroville. Since it was not a part of the planned city, it was decided to get rid of it and build Bharat Nivas there. That's one interpretation.

So with a couple of people who had been living in Silence, we started a new settlement called Kottakarai, simply named after the adjacent village. For the first couple of months, I worked at Matrimandir, where we were excavating that first hole, which kept on shifting in the beginning. And then once we moved to Kottakarai, I got into working with the land. Kottakarai community was set up by digging an open well to start a tree nursery. The tree nursery was supposed to provide trees for Bharat Nivas. That's how we got into tree planting, because when all those seedlings were ready, nobody wanted to plant trees around Bharat Nivas, because it would spoil the view of the beautiful architecture. As we had all these hundreds of trees on our hands, we decided to look around in Kottakarai and see where they could be planted. As a result, we planted the most amazing trees in the most unsuitable places. They were almost all ornamentals and definitely not all indigenous. Most of them were exotic and not hardy at all, so the survival rates were extremely low. The places where we planted also contributed. The Alankuppam tank, for instance - after planting we found out it was a major grazing area for the surrounding villages. So these were our first beginnings of afforestation. Nobody knew anything about afforestation anyway, we just learned by trial and error, and by doing it.

Francis

As Jaap explained, we made enormous mistakes at the beginning, all of us not knowing anything about what we were doing. Then it just slowly got more organized, and we'd evolved more, and the numbers started to increase, and the nurseries started popping up, and all of a sudden thousands of trees were going in every year. They were just little sticks in the ground, and today it's a beautiful forest.

Joss

We now know 400 plants in this area that have medicinal properties. We now can see that we have done a lot. And what is 27 years in terms of a forest?

Jaap

We settled somewhere and saw land around us, and realized that maybe it would make sense to grow some of our own food, grow cow grass and vegetables. Oh there's another field where we can grow some grains, it's a bit windy, maybe we need some trees as wind protection and shade. We grew into it naturally, and for years we learned from our neighbours in the surrounding villages. That's where we picked up all our knowledge about how to deal with the land, what the patterns were, the seasons, what happened at what time of the year. And the afforestation thing, as Francis said, only became organized over the years. At first, it was a very haphazard sort of thing, as we had no idea what we were doing. We just saw the need to plant some trees, and we basically planted everything we could lay our hands on.

Over the years we learned that there are certain characteristics in trees which need to be taken into account, so they would have a better chance of survival. We started introducing exotics that turned out to be extremely hardy, gradually started looking at forests around us, got interested in planting timber trees, and fruit trees of course. But until this day I only know of one person who came here with some background that had to do with trees or afforestation. For the rest, to my knowledge, everyone else just learned the trade by doing it here, without any prior experience.

Charlie

The only person I knew at the beginning who really knew something about trees was Narad *(founder of the Matrimandir Nursery, presently lives in USA, and visits Auroville often)*. Horticulture was his thing. He knew a lot. He was the expert. He was not really doing forestry then, but in the beginning he provided many of the trees that went out into Auroville for forestry. The first year we knew nothing, and yet it was logical that to grow a tree you have to take a seed, dig a hole, and put it in, but we also put in wrong types of trees, used wrong methods, planted at wrong times.

We didn't understand what the climate was like here. We knew it was hot, but we didn't understand what a monsoon was. I know my first monsoon set my head as to what I thought a monsoon was like for so many years. It finally dawned on me, after about twelve or thirteen years, that the monsoon is a season when the rain will come. And it may be this much rain, or that much rain, and it may come at the beginning, or it may come at the end or in the middle of the season, or have a hole in the centre. And actually, the monsoon is not what it was the first year I was here.

Joss

Just like Jaap said, in those years we were watching the sun come up and go down, and feeling the temperature, and the wind, and learning what the conditions were. We were definitely pretty low key. We had our donkeys, and we made our own bullock carts and then drove them. We had to learn to plough our fields as well as the guy across the fence. Otherwise they'd laugh at you. And this was very important in those times. My real contact with the village came after Forecomers, when I went to live just on the outskirts of Kuilapalayam, when I built the television studio and a house almost where the Dental Clinic is today. That's all there was. There was Aspiration on one side and we were just on the outskirts of the village, between the village and Fraternity. And then we were interacting almost all the time. They were our teachers for so much and it is from them that we were learning particularly how to grow food.

What I mentioned before was that often when you came out to Auroville, particularly in the rainy season, it was this sea of green. I like to remember this reality too, and I think I am right, that then at that time, there was certainly more food grown on the plateau of Auroville and consumed here in those early years than is grown now. Now what is grown on the plateau is cashew nuts, and that is an exotic export crop.

Later when I started Pitchandikulam in 1973, I had to relate to the local farmers. It was important when starting a new place. They were perhaps the formal watchmen of the area, where you came to a dynamic edge with your neighbor, when you started putting up fences. And this is a country where there were no fences here then. And suddenly we say, "hey, we'd like to conduct our experiment on this side of the fence, and you go on with yours on that side, your goats and cows and whatever." And there's a certain dynamic edge there that leads to kattis at your throats, and all sorts of stuff. In that first year of Pitchandikulam, as well as planting 50,000 trees, we grew 40 bags of *oolandu*, 20 bags of *ragi and samai*, these are all local grains. We did incredible harvests, and Jaap was doing the same over on Kottakarai side.

And we were growing food, and it was particularly through the food that we related to the farmers. The farmers weren't planting trees. They said, "what do you mean? It is fine to plant jackfruit or mango or casuarina, but none of this other strange stuff." We had already perhaps 60 or 70 species in our nursery that we were planting. However the villages very much respected us in those early years, because we were farming, because we were doing dry-land farming with them. If today we were growing a lot of dry-land crops over the Auroville plateau and over the Auroville land, and were very much more self-sufficient in that way, I think we'd have a lot more respect now.

Charlie

The land was in terrible condition. Actually the agriculture that the villagers had been following had led to the edge of the total destruction of this land. There were a lot of bad practices going on, but not to blame the villagers themselves. During the summer, all you saw was red, and there were incredible dust storms going on. That was in part because of the agricultural practices. It's very difficult to do monsoon agriculture, and you have to praise the way they were managing. And they had to. Otherwise they starved. Many people in the village really did not have any other source of income or food, except for what they grew. I don't know if people were starving, but people sometimes only ate one meal a day in the bad years.

So under the difficult conditions where all the biomass of the whole area had been destroyed, they had nothing to put in the land except something from their own animals, cow dung.

Under the short monsoon period, for example, they were doing one practice which always hit me really strong. After the agricultural season was finished, if there was a good rain, many farmers would plough their land. It made good sense in one way. Why did they do it? They wanted to kill every weed that was on the land, so that when the next rainy season would come, they could start their agriculture instantly. They would just plough the already barren land. This sort of practice had left what was on the edge of a desert. There were actually sand storms. The soil was washing away.

So when we came here, it was obvious we had to do something. There were canyons all over. There are still canyons today, but then they were totally out of control. I remember we had big canyons in Forecomers, and all the soil from the farmers' fields was all there in one of the canyons, and we would just take it and smear it on ourselves. It was actually really medicinal.

Francis

As was explained earlier, they were farming for existence. We were coming here out of a somewhat middle class 60's background, with no need to farm for our livelihood. We were two opposing cultures, totally, on the economic level, as well as the cultural level. Probably, the first confrontational situation was when we started to put up fences, so their cows and goats could no longer graze freely over our lands. We were trying to have the growth produce and save itself, so we could finally have some topsoil on our land, and just through lots of talking, compromising, sometimes screaming at each other, we worked it out.

Charlie

I think the villagers in the beginning thought we were nuts to come here. Why would we come here if we could be somewhere else, but I think there was some respect for us also, particularly if we were able to do the farming a bit. Of course we weren't very good farmers, so they probably thought it was a bit of a laugh, but as far as the tree planting went, they thought we were nuts.

Kanniyappan

I don't know what others thought about it, but what I remember is mainly in Auroville, people were doing afforestation. People wondered why planting only trees. Why not crops and fruit trees?

It would be useful to sell, and get some money. Planting trees, you only spend money. They wondered where it came from, and how they managed.

Joss

There were a lot of really good times and good relationships with the people in the village. I started Pitchandikulam with a group of young kids from the village. We just went there and camped under a tree, and that was it. It was just me and these village kids. In that first year a lot of the trees that we grew, went out to village lands.

In those early years, there was a great demand for mangoes and jackfruits. Even the cashews, a lot of cashews were planted from the Auroville nurseries. There was a lot of sharing too. By the next year we were starting to plant on village lands. We started to plant 'the avenue' *(road from Certitude to Kuilapalayam), the perombokes*, and this was something that we had to work out with the village elders. Then it wasn't so much the *panchayat*, but it was the elders, because then the village still had a very solid structure of elders.

Then there were questions about the village pond, so we worked a lot on the village pond and dug it out deeper. And we worked out which trees to plant up the road, and which trees to plant on the Pitchandikulam peromboke in conjunction with them, with a deal that we would protect it with fences for three years. At the end of this period we would take the fences away, so cows and goats and people could go through, which they do today.

There was a lot of relationship with the village, because there was just the village, and we all had accounts in the village teashop. There were no Auroville shops. If you needed some beedies you went down to the village shop. Building good relations with the villagers was one of the main objectives of Kottakarai, a community with the same name as the adjacent village.

Lisbeth

There was Auroville land near Kottakarai. You see, at that time you wouldn't look, as you look now, for a big space, as far away from the villages as possible. At that time, you wanted to be a bit protected. There were no trees. And since we knew the villagers in Kottakarai, and we were working with them, for us this was very attractive, these few lands near Kottakarai village, and we asked Mother whether we could start there. She said, "Yes, you can, but it is very important, if you live so close to the village, to work with the villagers."

Ramachandaran from Kottakarai

First the Auroville people were purchasing lands from Kottakarai village. People were afraid to sell their lands, because they might all be evicted. Even my own uncle said not to sell lands, that only destitute people sell land to Auroville. But slowly some people started selling land to Auroville. *(translated from Tamil by Varadharajan)*

Lisbeth

We were physically working really hard. We had some villagers to help us, but at that time I think the relationship with the villagers was very nice. We were really working together physically, really hard.

Varadharajan

When these Westerners came, it gave these local people a certain work culture, which is very good. They were working on the land, and they also used to work along with the villagers, whereas in India the manager does not work along with the workers. He assumes a superior position, and will always work above them.

Lisbeth

We had no electricity in Kottakarai for many years, and so the water was pulled out by buckets from the well, put in barrels on the vandi, and so all the trees were watered. Sometimes you would come in the morning, and find all your trees, that were half a year old, and very carefully nurtured, just gone, either pulled out or eaten by goats. It was very hard, so we got wise, and got a watchman, who watched the trees.

This actually was how our tree planting started, and later we got some cows, and our own bullock cart, and some chickens, and a vegetable garden, and built a community. The first bakery *(in Auroville)* was started in Kottakarai by Larry *(an early Aurovilian who now lives in USA)* with Sundaram, who is now in Village Action. In fact they just had a barrel. That was the first oven.

Water delivery for early communities

Forecomers
Fraternity

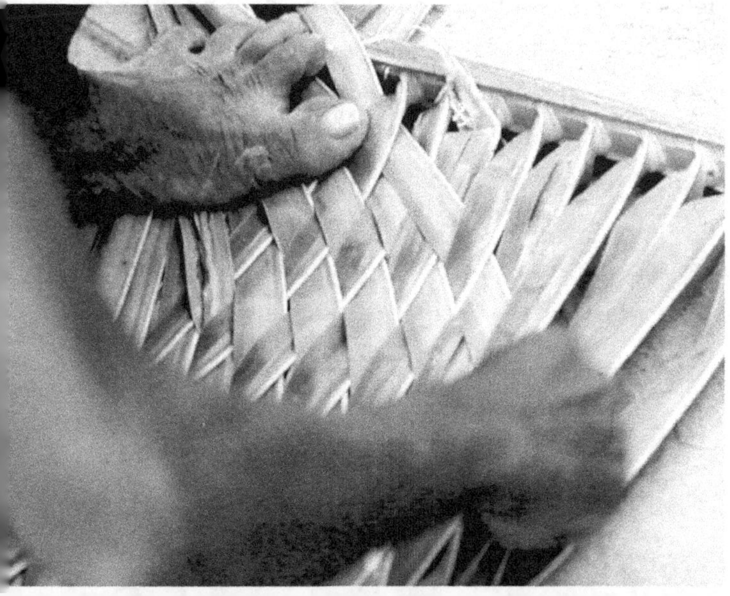

Jocelyn

At Kottakarai, the relationship with the village was just totally incredible. I mean, Constance *(early Aurovilian who now lives in USA)* moved right into the middle of Kottakarai village, and he lived in a little, tiny loft, really small, with Iris and Mitra, and downstairs there was a clinic. And there was an intimacy with the village that I haven't seen existing elsewhere, very close friends, people who really cared about each other. Bhoomadevi *(an Aurovilian originally from Kottakarai)* was like part of the family. Everything was shared in the community. A lot of Tamil workers became Aurovilian in the Kottakarai community, at that point. They are still members of the community. There was a complete equality, and there was no ownership. I mean this wasn't my field, and your field. The community shared the responsibility for an area. It was a different consciousness.

Lisbeth

Over the years everything has so rapidly changed. This was a time when we started this little clinic in the village. It was an ayurvedic clinic, and at that time the old ayurvedic physician of the Ashram was still alive, and he used to come every Sunday, and see the cases that we had questions about.

Village life was really tough at these times. I remember the case of a mother, who had a small baby. That mother and I did some work on crocheted carpets, and together with Daniel *(an early Aurovilian who now lives in USA and Mexico)*, we made some hammocks, and coloured and dyed them. This mother's baby died, and we found out that it was because she sold her breast milk to the teashop. These things really happened. People were very poor. But somehow with Constance, who lived right inside the village, and we lived right on the edge of the wadi, we started a beautiful bamboo playground there. Once, we left for two weeks, and when we came back the whole playground had disappeared, as firewood. But in any case, we had a good relationship. Mother said that it was very important to work with the villagers. We also had a snack program, where we served kadalai, and bananas to the kids. We had a sports program, and this little ayurvedic clinic. As Jocelyn said, a lot of these Tamil people in the village became Aurovilian.

For me, this is a time that was so joyful, basically because Mother was always there to give us guidance. It was hard, physically hard to live and work here, but the people were happy, open. It was just a very wonderful time.

Ramachandaran

First I was working with Daniel. At that time Aurovilians used to get Prosperity from the office in Pondicherry. Prosperity means that every month, whatever the needs of the people were, they would be given through the Prosperity section. So we used to go to Pondicherry and get all the Prosperity items. *(translated from Tamil by Varadharajan)*

Lisbeth

There was more sharing. For instance, there was this man called Murugesan *(passed away in 2010)*. He had a family. He later became Aurovilian, but before he became Aurovilian, he was working not for us, but with us, and we shared seeds. We planted varagu and red rice, all the old grains were still eaten by the villagers. There was no electricity in Kottakarai village. Marriages were not big affairs, with big loud speakers or big cinemas. There would be the classical musicians there playing the music. It was quiet. There were no motorcycles.

Ramachandaran

In the Western culture, as far as we have seen from Auroville, a man and a woman just live together, and separate very frequently, which is not very acceptable in Tamil culture, and should not happen as frequently as that in the atmosphere here. That is the thing I found difficult to accept. But it is your culture, it is your way. During my grandfather's time there was no Auroville. People were very old fashioned, and now it is entirely different. After Auroville came, so many people learned about handicrafts. They became technicians and craftsmen. I work as an electrician in the electrical service, and am very well qualified now, good experience. *(translated from Tamil by Varadharajan)*

Lisbeth

We worked. That was what we were here for. People didn't go out every year to Europe or America. They stayed here. They stayed here for years. If there was a family emergency, such as your father, or close relative, being very ill, you would go, but otherwise people stayed. People, with the kind of enthusiasm that we had, don't seem to come to Auroville anymore. Now it's all planned, and do I have enough money in the bank to build my house, and buy my motorcycle or moped, and this and that. I mean, that is just such another concept for coming here, and this is very often hard for us to take.

Excavation at Matrimandir, Beginning of Matrimandir Nursery, and Bharat Nivas

Mother's blessing for the Matrimandir

Matrimandir inauguration exhibition under the Banyan Tree

Starting with many separate holes...

...later 400 payed diggers were brought in to complete the excavation

On Mother's birthday, 21st February 1971 the foundation stone was laid for the Matrimandir, and a nursery was started for the Matrimandir Gardens. Some of the people, who organized the work there, were travelers, who just happened to arrive at the right moment.

Amrit in the Matrimandir nursery

Matrimandir kitchen

Amrit in the Matrimandir nursery

Matrimandir kitchen

Michael Tait

Knowing that Auroville was 10 kilometres or so from Pondicherry, I walked down the beach from Madras *(now Chennai)*, and when I saw the lights of Pondicherry, I stopped and spent the night. In the morning I walked up into Auroville, and I had various adventures trying to find a place to stay in Auroville, and I think I ended up that night right next to where Matrimandir is now, in a wooden storage shed, where there was a spare bed. Someone offered that I spend the night in that shed, which later became part of Fidelity. Now it is called Shanti. I think there's also a house there now. That was on the 15th February, and a few days later I was asked to help prepare the foundation ceremony of this Matrimandir. I knew nothing about Auroville. I hadn't read anything. I hadn't heard anything except that this place existed. I saw Shyamsundar *(appointed by the Mother to be liaison between her and Auroville; he passed away in 2011)* and Namas *(early Aurovilian from USA, who died several years ago)* washing these pebbles which were going to be used to concrete this foundation stone in the ground. So my first job was washing pebbles with this swami-model Indian, Shyamsundar, who in those days was actually in charge of Auroville. So sitting on the ground washing pebbles was the first thing I did.

Piero

After the first idea of the Matrimandir, of the vision of the inner room, came from the Mother, about one year passed before the project became more clear, and began to manifest. On the 21st February 1971, it was decided to lay the first stone. There was the ceremony, and it was decided to lay the stone far from the center of the building, because after the excavation would have gone deeper, it would have been a problem to keep this place safe. The place, that was chosen, was near the banyan, but nobody remembers anymore where it is. It was buried, and then it disappeared. The ceremony was with a rich participation from the Ashram, and from Auroville; maybe a thousand people came.

The funny thing was that the day after this ceremony, there was nobody anymore on the spot. There was the idea to wait until the contractor would show up and all that. So it was the sort of initiative of a few Aurovilians, who heroically and stoically decided to start digging, without knowing where the building was to come, only guided by I don't know what, the sun, the stars, by some intuition about where the place was. In any case the excavation was supposed to be very big, so wherever a small or big digging was happening, was not very relevant.

Tapas

It remained in the back of my mind, that one day I should come, and discover this place. It happened finally in 1971, when there was the inaugural ceremony of Matrimandir foundation. I used to come, with a group of Ashram members, on the bus to help for the digging on a regular basis. It was an outing for us from the Ashram to come out, and have the collective experience of working together. It was really fun. Whenever there would be an event, I would make sure I was there.

Larry Nagel

Larry (right) with Diane and Auralice as a baby

Actually I was on the way to Madurai to see the temples there, but in Pondicherry I happened to go to the Samadhi, and actually had a very peaceful experience there. But just when I looked up, I ran into somebody, actually the one Indian person I'd known before, that I went to university with.

He happened to be there, and he kind of collared me, and took me across the street, and bought me a few books, and got a bicycle, and took me out to Auroville. It was late March '71, and what I remember specifically about that first day was that I was very attracted by all the surroundings. It was very barren, but there was something about it that I took to right away, and I had this feeling that I'd like to help out.

I didn't know much about the concept of Auroville, and certainly not about the concept of Matrimandir. I was near the center of Auroville by the Banyan, and there was somebody there, so I said, "Well, I think I'll be around here to help with something, if there's anything anybody needs help with."

It turned out that the next morning was when they began excavating at the Matrimandir. So, I showed up the next morning, and like Piero said, it was a very intriguing and beautiful experience, because you had these people from all over, and all different ages, and all different inclinations.

Basically, we would be digging earth, and putting it in little pans on our head, and moving it from one place to the other. For the first time I felt I was doing something that I was actually supposed to be doing, even though I really wasn't sure what it was all about.

It actually drew me to try to understand who this woman called the Mother was, that I had only heard of when I came. I only met her after I had been working a couple of months. I feel somehow that the communal involvement, that everybody throughout Auroville, with all our differences, was somehow involved in, and that was going on every day right at the physical level, was what was needed at the time to get Auroville spiritually off the ground. I just know that for me it was a very, very powerful experience. I've probably doubted everything I've done in life, except working there. That was something that I knew was a very precious thing for me to do, and to be a part of.

Piero

The observation of Larry is true, there were the strongest characters in Auroville all concentrated there, and also because of their characters, each one was digging a separate hole. And it was going on, digging, digging and this earth would be moved to somewhere, but not knowing exactly where. That was the early heroism, without knowing exactly what the purpose of doing it was. That lasted till October of the same year. Well, I started to be busy with Matrimandir only when these guys started digging. And there were other people, who were concerned with what do we do now, or what do we do next, and only then did I become directly involved.

My first participation was only just witnessing what was happening, reading the conversations between Mother and Satprem, and looking. But when people started to seriously question if we could build the Matrimandir ourselves, if we could in some way avoid having to deal with a contractor, who was coming for profit, and with the idea of using mass labour and so on, was the point where I just wanted to state that it was possible. I would work out the program for doing the foundation of the construction and the four pillars, postponing the decision for the rest, till after the pillars were finished. That was the question that was put to Mother in October '71. Can we start like that? We have to remember that we were not having the money to attract a big contractor. A contractor would have asked immediately for one third of the amount, going for big money. Fundraising was just starting, and the means necessary for the foundation were not so big, and we would have started slowly, with the amount of materials that we were able to buy. So that was the question that was put to the Mother. And the letter was compiled with a rough explanation on how to do the work. And then, when the answer came from the Mother, "yes very good", there was the feeling from many people that now we should start. And then we started to organize the work.

Immediately after one week the counter order came, and that was the typical thing of Matrimandir. No, no, no, Mother has decided to take a contractor, what do you guys want to do here? So that postponed things a little bit, and then there were messages up and down for some time.

Gloria

I remember, in the beginning she said, "yes" for the contractor, and then somebody else asked her if maybe it would be better for villagers, and she said, "yes, yes, very good." So then we asked her, "what?" and she said, "I am not an expert to judge in technical matters, but I know with goodwill one can always come to an agreement." She left the solution to the experts.

Michael T

Well, at that point moving the earth was the only job going. No doubt Piero was slaving away at mental work, but the only physical job was picking at the earth, moving the earth.

Then, of course, there was a long period when there was very little work for the coolies at Matrimandir, because 400 villagers were brought in, and the excavation was done by the villagers.

Piero

Here in India, there were these special digging teams, who worked on contract. Sometimes they would come from very far, and in our case, there were some gangs of workers that were coming from Andhra Pradesh, for example. They knew where there was a big construction work, and they appeared there to get this digging work on contract.

Michael T

It was one of the most beautiful things I remember having ever seen. You've seen the pictures, especially in the moonlight, of the excavation with the steps where the workers moved up and down, I mean it was like an anthill. It was like you imagined the pyramids. It was actually a very, very moving and inspiring thing to see this hole being made by these lines of four or five hundred men, which I think was the maximum number.

Then there were half a dozen people, who with theodolites would check that the digging was done correctly. That period, when a group of unskilled people could come together at will and work, was over for a while, while the excavation was being done. During that period, I actually went to Bharat Nivas because the construction had started there, and I was one of the Aurovilians, who liaised with the construction team. So, I had an experience of what Piero is talking about, the concept of bringing in an outside construction company, which was used for putting up huge buildings, and having them construct a building in Auroville. Only when the steel work started actually on the mud mat at the bottom of the excavation did it become possible for anybody to turn up for group activities there again.

Larry

At Matrimandir I started with the excavation, and then there was a period where the work at the Nursery was kind of combined, because we were preparing the Nursery for the Matrimandir. I divided my day. I was half day at the Nursery and half day at Matrimandir.

Michael T

The greatest diggers were really resentful that people from the Nursery could come and try to steal some of the coolies away.

Joss

Narad was coming out to Marakkanam, spending days there. He was also going to all of the botanical gardens of India. There were a lot of details, even then, of how the forest would join up to the city, and the Matrimandir Gardens, and the green corridors, and things like that.

Kanniyappan

At that time, my father was working in the Matrimandir Nursery, so when I had free time, I came to see what they were doing, and then slowly I got interested in the forest, working with all these trees and plants. It continued for some time like that, and then Narad gave me a job watering the plants. I liked that job, to play with the water. It was really fun to do that job.

Chapter 5, 1972

Work on the four Pillars of Matrimandir

Piero

The first concreting was in February '72. That was the real first stone, one of these pieces of petrified wood that is found somewhere in the canyon. Somebody had flattened it on one side, and Mother has signed with a beautiful 'AUM' ॐ that was afterwards photographed. We only keep the remembrance from the photograph, because the actual stone remained in the foundation. It was a nice beginning, the true beginning. It was shared by so many people, maybe 2000 people that came. There was a long line of persons, and each one would take one or more stones from the pile of gravel for the concreting, and put them into the mixing machine. Each person passing in front was doing that with a different aim, a different inspiration. For some persons, to put this stone in the machine was like their whole life. For others it was just throwing in a little bit of gravel. So anyhow there was brought in a first concreting machine that was lowered down and was used for cementing this small stone in the foundation of the east pillar.

Meanwhile, another letter went to Mother from my side to ask her if we had to go on in the same way with Aurovilians, or would we finally get the decision for a contractor. In this second case, the answer of Mother was very clear and immediate. "You continue like now." So that was the confirmation that the work was done properly. We were then engaged in a major construction, which actually kept me busy for another 18 years.

There were natural talents that were showing up, and were taking the job quite seriously. I think we were quite fortunate, and in these cases I don't think that you have to teach anyone. I think actually the best is not to teach anybody, because if we start teaching, people pretend to know, and then it's even worse. It's better to let things happen, and then, slowly guiding, watching, and being there the whole time, to explain exactly the small steps that have to be done. It's more effective, and then later people start to grasp the whole of the work. Then it becomes easier, as they can start to read the drawing, and start to understand more.

Michael T

What Piero said earlier about supposedly intelligent people in this huge construction, we never saw it that way, because it was never like concrete, and so we put steel on top of the concrete, and it was almost only when we were half way up that we began to realize what we had built.

There was never the feeling that we were undertaking this huge building, because I think for many of us, we never saw what the thing would become. We'd seen the model of the galaxy, with this thing with drawing pins on it in the middle, the beautiful model that Roger had made of the galaxy. But none of us really knew what we were building.

I left Matrimandir in '79 and went into other things, and when I came back a few years later, and tried to climb up where I used to work, hanging on by one hand out in space, it blew my mind. But when you'd reach that point by every day going up a little bit, you never realize how high you are. So, the building was like that. None of us realized what we were doing, because it was a day-to-day thing. There was never any question of why, or we're not qualified to do that. Of course we were qualified, if someone says to tie the ends of steel in this shape, any one of us could do it.

Piero

Everything, in the beginning, went quite fast. The problems came later with the question of the Sri Aurobindo Society, and when the whole finance was in doubt.

Michael T

At one point, when I was doing most of the purchasing in Madras, and I would go to Shyamsundar and say, "look, we need five tons of steel and ten lorries of cement."

Shyamsundar would scratch his head, and the next day he would come with an envelope with the cash, and we would go to Madras. And it was literally hand to mouth like that. We didn't know where the next thing was going to come from, but I don't think it ever slowed down the work.

Piero

Here it's very hot and for the benefit of the concrete, not for the benefit of the workers, it's better to do the concreting at night. We were in need of labour for the night work, so we were sending word around, and even from Pondicherry we got such a beautiful response. Many people were coming at six o'clock when we started, and they were working till one or two o'clock in the morning. For this huge concreting in the foundation, when the work was lasting many, many hours, sometimes we had a hundred or maybe a hundred and fifty persons working with the spot-light, and clamping it down, and then going and running around with the wheel-barrow. It was a nice atmosphere, full of enthusiasm.

Michael T

The workers had worked all day long, you must remember. Then they'd go and have a cup of tea, and then have 8 hours of concreting. That was the way it used to be.

Larry

I mostly remember this experience of putting the concrete beams on, when we were working late; it was never a feeling of we're going to build this building. As Michael said it was what was going to be done that day with whoever was there. That was another very interesting thing. We had crews that Piero trained, it was kind of like somebody learned from him, and then passed it on. The crews would change completely from one day to the next. And that was a very beautiful thing, because we would be all sorts of people, and it always seemed to work. This is coming from somebody, who was just working on a daily basis. That was incredibly beautiful. And then especially when we had these concretings, and everybody would come, and it would go on through the night. There's nothing I've ever done before or after, that can compare to the joy of participating in things like that.

Piero

Laying the floor

Laying the floor

21st February 1972

Steelwork for the pillars

In those early times, the team on site was not really big; it was mainly meant to prepare the work for the concreting, so we were preparing the steel and the shuttering work. For the shuttering wood work, I was counting on a team of local carpenters, because the work was more specialized, and it was not easy to get Aurovilians doing that. So, with that in mind, maybe there were on-site 30 or 40 people, not more than that.

On the days of the concreting, which was normally once a week, or a little bit longer when it was necessary, we were using a hundred people, or

Completion of the four pillars

a hundred and twenty people. One of the essential things was not to get rain during the concreting, so that was always the challenge during the monsoon time. What do we do now? We would look at the sky, maybe in the morning it would rain, and now what to do? And then people were running to the Ashram, and sending the message to the Mother. "We are concreting today; give us a day without rain." And in fact, we have always been able to avoid major problems, or any problem with rain. It's remarkable, especially when we were doing concreting for the foundation. In certain cases we have worked for 24 hours and more, continuously.

This period here was also important, because we were keeping a thread with the Mother. The construction was going on, but on the day of the concreting, suddenly, we were in the blessing of the Mother. There was a bunch of flowers coming, somebody from the Ashram was coming and was bringing things that were sent by Mother to go into the concreting. That was the sort of thread there was. Actually I always felt like the Mother was following the construction much more than the chief architect. She was there when the concreting was done. We were perceiving that more concretely than anything else in small things like these small blessings packets. They were so sweet, arriving at the right moment.

They were passed almost secretly. This has been sent by Mother, and she wants you to put this in the concrete. And then we were doing that at the right moment without ceremony. It was just there happening.

Michael T

We had a storeroom and some tools, and we had these vibrators, and we had the concrete mixer. And then there was a major catastrophe when the concrete mixer broke down. A mechanic came from Calcutta *(now Kolkata)*, and he looked at the mixer, and said that certain parts had to be replaced.

It happened, by the grace, that when the concrete mixer was broken, there were no major concretings to be done. So suddenly I was responsible for getting this concrete mixer running again with the mechanic from Calcutta.

I did that job, and then Jack Alexander *(early Aurovilian who now lives in USA and visits Auroville regularly)* came from America with a container load of tools, all sorts of nice do-it-yourself tools and a craftsman's lathe. He picked them up in garage-sales and whatever in America. Then we built a keeth shed for these tools, and then we started playing with these tools. Piero wanted more wheel-barrows made, so we started making wheel-barrows. It evolved like that.

There was a cyclone at the end of December '72, and quite a few buildings in Matrimandir, which were keeth buildings, were destroyed. The roofs fell over, and in the workshop we found that we had to dismantle everything right down to the bearings, because forced inside the machine right into the bearings were bits of keeth. The wind had been so strong. At that point I went to Shyamsundar and said, "it's ridiculous, you can't build Matrimandir with a keeth workshop; we need a proper workshop." So he raised the money, and Piero did the design, and we put up what is now the nexus of the workshop, an asbestos building.

From that day onwards, I was in the workshop more than on the construction site. So again, it was something with no conscious decision, it was just how things evolved in Matrimandir. We evolved into a speciality or a job, like Auroville today where everything is evolving, and Matrimandir is like that. At that point, I bought and read a lot of books on engineering, and mechanics. For the things I needed to know, I would go through a book and just stop at the chapters, which seemed relevant to Matrimandir. That's how the workshop started, basically. We had a combination of Aurovilians who would work in the workshop and tambis like Ramalingam *(long time Aurovilian)*. Local tambis would somehow get attracted, and come and work, and you'd show them what to do. As we learned, they learned.

Kalyamurthy from Edayanchavadi

I had studied up to fifth standard and then come to Auroville for work. I was about ten years old when my father died. I was working in Matrimandir. At that time there used to be three shifts where people used to work. *(translated from Tamil by Varadharajan)*

Unlike today, when most children in the villages around Auroville attend school, in the 60's and 70's, the opposite was true. Most children tended the goats and cows, or helped their families with household chores. If their relatives worked in Auroville they would come to deliver their lunch boxes and hang out, curious about what was going on, all new and interesting for them. Some enjoyed helping out, and by acquiring new skills they slowly grew into Auroville. Many of them are still here.

Michael T

The experience, particularly in '72, which was Sri Aurobindo's centenary, was so powerful that, when people asked how we could work in those environments, it was grace to work in those environments. There was no suffering involved, it was a total grace.

Larry

It was a total grace. But also for me, because I was just beginning then to get an understanding of, and involved in, the yoga of Sri Aurobindo, for me it was a real introduction to karma yoga in a very physical sense, which was a very important thing for me to learn in such a magical situation. I'm very grateful.

Chapter 6, 1973

The Mother Leaves Her Body

Mother's Mahasamdhi.
Photo courtesy Sri Aurobindo Ashram Archives, Pondicherry.

On 17th November 1973 the Mother left her body around 7:00 in the evening. The message reached Auroville the morning of the 18th, and in complete shock, everybody from Auroville rushed to the Ashram in Pondicherry.

Aster

The 20th evening was a totally different and new experience. The body had been laid in the structure of the Samadhi in the central courtyard of the Ashram, and late evening I entered the Ashram to go close to it. And that simple structure seemed to explode, not in any metaphorical sense, but in a most concrete visual sense, in the most concrete sense of the dynamism and the vibrations that emanated from it. The simple rectangular structure on the ground, from the base where the joints were, seemed almost lifted up a little bit from the ground, with a rush of force emanating from it, a force of joy, of fulfillment, of a fullness that the structure of the Samadhi could not contain, and totally impregnated with a white light that came out. I was stunned and stopped short a few steps from the Samadhi. This must have been the one experience that nothing in my being could have anticipated.

Not that I had anticipated anything. One wasn't in that phase of consciousness at the moment. But that fullness, that dynamism, that something which escaped it physically and otherwise, is with me today. I can't explain it. I don't understand it any better today than I did in '73.

Michael Z

I experienced an atmosphere of such solid pressure in the Ashram compound, and all over, that day. It was like something absolutely dense and solid pressing down on one. I don't even know how to describe it. It was just force. As I remember, it wasn't particularly blissful, or painful, or anything. It was just sheer dense, solid force and the feeling that this wasn't just a subjective experience; this was in the atmosphere and anyone, who was there, could have felt this thing. It just enveloped one. I sat for I don't know how many hours during that day in the Ashram compound, and there was just this experience of force pressing down, pressing down, pressing down. Occasionally the experience was as if one was in between this force and surrounded by this force, and every sort of now and then, it just sort of closed, and one disappeared into it.

Then it would be released again, and one would be left with this feeling of pressure. I wasn't thinking very much about it at the time, but it was quite clear that Mother's force wasn't at all diminished by the fact that she had left her body. If anything, this was the most absolutely unquestionable demonstration of sheer force that could be imagined.

Aster

In 1950, a month after Sri Aurobindo left the body, Mother called a national convention to start a major educational venture. And in the two or three years that followed, there was such an external expansion of Sri Aurobindo's work, and in that context, Mother had said the consciousness is freer in scope, wider in amplitude for its action, without the body.

I cannot say if one can re-quote this in later years, but certainly a whole new way of being with the Mother was what we were given.

With that new way of being with the Mother, which is perhaps the simplest and best way I can formulate it, a new direction of experience started. Something in the physical, something in the presence in the physical, molding it, changing it, which was not there before, and which carries something, and which, in fact, is very largely instrumental for putting me right in the midst of the experience of Auroville.

Completion of the Four Pillars of Matrimandir

16th November 1973. Jaap, Raman and Ruud (from left)

End tip of the pillars after their shuttering removal

17.11.1973 in the morning
Photo courtesy Sri Aurobindo Ashram Archives, Pondicherry.

The concreting of the "first slab" which joins the 4 pillars had taken place between 11th and 14th November. What was missing were the tips of the pillars, 8 small triangular pieces which rise above the first slab.

17.11.1973 in the night

Piero

It so happened that we just cast the last tip of the fourth and last pillar on the same day and in the same hour that Mother left her body. So it was symbolically the completion of the four aspects of the Mother that were cast into concrete.

Author's Note

Author's Note

The interviews presented in this book are part of a history program for newcomers that I had created with my friend, Philip Melville in 1997. The plan was to divide Auroville's history into different eras and then interview Aurovilians according to their area of knowledge. Our first section would cover the years from 1968 till 1973 when the Mother was still in her physical body.

Sally Champe was a newcomer in 1997 and we asked her to do the interviews and Vladimir Yatsenko to do the video recording. At that time digital recording was very new, and hardly happening in Auroville. Vladimir used an analogue camera and the interviews were recorded on video tape.

We made 10 group conversations, which I transcribed over the next few months. We then took a break, before starting the next part, which would have been about our struggles and eventual break with the Sri Aurobindo Society.

However for reasons which I no longer remember, we did not resume working on this project and the video tapes stayed in a cupboard for the next 8 or 9 years.

In 2004 I came across the videos again. Peter Thurrel gave me an old television set, which had an attachment for watching videos. Loretta Shartsis and I watched them together and thought we had enough material to make an interesting documentary. We went to the archives and copied many old photos to support the content. Meanwhile I searched everywhere for someone who could digitize the tapes. Finally B Sullivan took them to the USA, and eventually found a person in Canada, who was able to do the job.

By this point Loretta was not able to continue so I put the project on hold again. In 2017 I showed the CDs to Kati Hötger. We discovered that the tapes had deteriorated badly over the years. However we still had the transcriptions of these vivid and inspiring conversations about our very early days, so we decided to present them in this book, which would describe what happened between 1968 and 1973.

I am grateful for all the support I received to give birth to this book. My special thank you goes to: Kati Hötger for working with me on this book over two long years; Pranav Kumar for the development and design of the book and this web book; Doris van Kalker and Digital Archives of Auroville for providing many of the pictures; and Prisma Books and Franz Fassbender for embarking on the adventure of this first web book of / on Auroville, and for publishing the book.

~ Janet Fearn, Late 2020

Author

JANET FEARN left her job as a psychiatric social worker in Toronto, Canada to travel around the world. She arrived in Pondicherry in June of 1968, stayed first in the Sri Aurobindo Ashram and then, in September, moved to Auroville. Over her 50+ years in Auroville, Janet painted pipes at the Matrimandir in the early days, ran a handicraft workshop, and later a guesthouse, and raised 2 children. She was also on a few different Auroville Councils, and more recently worked for some years with her daughter on the team of Restorative Circles, a community process for those in conflict. For Janet it never changed that she believes in Auroville and is happy being here.

Appendices

The people who were interviewed

People interviewed are listed alphabetically according to their first names. Surnames are given, except when the person observes the Tamil custom of using father's or husband's initial before his/her name. Most of the people interviewed are still living and working in Auroville.

Alok Aurovillian	: Lives in Auroville.
Ananda Reddy	: Lives in the Sri Aurobindo Ashram in Pondicherry.
Aster Patel	: Lives in Auroville
Bhaga (Christiane) Gabriau	: Lives in Auroville.
Charlie Lammert	: Lives in Auroville.
Christophe Pitoeff	: Lives in the Sri Aurobindo Ashram in Pondicherry.
Danielle (last name unknown)	: Danielle left Auroville around 69/70, and has made a few short visits since then.
S. Dhandapani	: Lives in Auroville.
Dorothee Hach	: Lives in Auroville.
Francis Neemberry	: Lives in Auroville
François Gautier	: Lives in Auroville
Gloria Buffi Cicionesi	: Lives in Auroville
Govindaraj	: From Kuilapalayam, passed away several years ago
Jaap den Hollander	: Lives in Auroville
Janet Fearn	: Lives in Auroville.
Jean-Claude Bieri	: No longer lives in Auroville, but is a regular visitor.
Jocelyn Shupack	: Lives in Auroville
Joss Brooks	: Divides his time between Auroville and his native Australia.
D. Kanniyappan	: Lost his life in a road accident in 2018.
Larry Nagel	: Lives in the USA, and is a regular visitor to Auroville.
Lisbeth Nusselein	: Lives in Auroville.
Kalyamurthy	: Lives in Edayanchavadi
Michael Tait	: Lives in Auroville.

Michael Zelnick	: Lives in Auroville.
Piero Cicionesi	: Lives in Auroville.
Poonga	: Lived in Kuilapalayam, passed away in 2014
Poppo (Reinhold) Pingel	: Lives in Auroville.
Prem Malik	: Passed away in 1999.
Ramachandaran	: Lives in Kottakarai
R. Ravi	: Lives in Auroville.
Savitra (Alan) Lithman	: Lives in the USA. Keeps in contact with many Aurovilians.
D. Selvaraj	: Lives in Auroville.
Shraddhavan (Maggie) Stuttle	: Lives in Auroville.
Tapas Bhatt	: Lives in Auroville.
G. Thillai	: Lives in Auroville.
G. Varadharajan	: Lives in Auroville.
Verne Henshall	: Lives in the USA and visits Auroville regularly.

Some words that are commonly used in Auroville

Tamil

Amma	:	woman, mother; colloquially also used for female employee
Ayurveda	:	ancient system of Indian medicine, still widely practiced
Beedi	:	cheap cigarette, made of unprocessed tobacco, wrapped in leaves
Bund	:	embankment to control the flow of water
Chappals	:	sandals
Coolie	:	labourer
Kadalai	:	chickpeas
Katti	:	knife
Keeth	:	woven coconut mat
Panchayat	:	an elected village council
Peromboke	:	lands belonging to the government
Swami	:	an ascetic, who has been initiated into a religious order
Tambi	:	small boy, little bother; colloquially also used for a young male helper
Vandi	:	bullock cart
Varagu	:	millet
Velakara	:	white person
Wadi	:	channel of a watercourse, which is dry except during rains

Sanskrit

Darshan	:	sight or appearance; sight of a guru (spiritual teacher) or a holy person
Samadhi	:	state of meditative consciousness or transcendent union; tomb of a saint or a holy person

Other

Pondy	:	common abbreviation for Pondicherry. The current name of Pondicherry is Puducherry

Other books published by PRISMA

Antithesis of Yoga
by Jocelyn

Finding the Psychic Being
by Loretta Shartsis

The Mother on Japan
by The Mother

The Teachings of Flowers
(The Life and Work of the Mother of the
Sri Aurobindo Ashram)
by Loretta Shartsis

Death doesn't exist
The Mother on Death, Sri Aurobindo on Rebirth
by The Mother

Passage to More than India
by Dick Batstone

The Supramental Transformation
by Loretta Shartsis

Children of Change: A Spiritual Pilgrimage
by Amrit

Memories of Auroville - told by early Aurovilians *by Janet
Fearn*

Bougainvilleas PROTECTION
by Narad (Richard Eggenberger), Nilisha Mehta

The Mother's Yoga - 1956-1973 (Vol. 1, 1956-1967) *by
Loretta Shartsis*

The Mother's Yoga - 1956-1973 (Vol. 2, 1968-1973) *by
Loretta Shartsis*

Crossroad The New Humanity
by Paulette Hadnagy